CRICUT MATERIALS

THE COMPLETE GUIDE TO ALL MATERIALS
SUPPORTED BY YOUR CRICUT MACHINE

Made with love

by

Sienna

Tally

Table of Contents

Introduction

First of all, thank you for purchasing this book. "Cricut Materials" is a guide for experts and beginners who want to expand their knowledge in the DIY industry. In writing this book, I did not particularly think about a specific type of Cricut machine. Creating this guide I wanted to create a kind of glossary of all materials compatible with all models of cricut released to date.
So here is a real encyclopedia for you lovers of "do it yourself". Description of materials, new discoveries and more.

If you are reading this book, it means you know what Cricut is and what it is used for. Perhaps it's the "how" that brought you here. However, for posterity's sake, Cricut is the brand name for an array of scrapbooking home cutters.
It is also the name used to categorize Provo Craft & Novelty Inc. projects, otherwise known as Provo Craft. Anyone who has these gizmos in their apartments uses them for various things, but particularly for cutting paper, felt, vinyl, fabrics, and other materials, including fondant.
Often, paper artisans have Cricut in their workshops alongside many other electronic cutting tools. You will also find this device with card makers and scrapbookers.
The machine has different models, inclusive of which is the Cricut Maker. This particular model is used in friendship with the Cricut

Design Space, cloud-based online software that will be the main focus of this book.

The software is not a lone wolf but needs an internet connection and a device - either a Personal Computer or smartphone. Be as that may, there is an offline version of Cricut Design Space you can use with your phone. Whether it's an Android device, iPad, or iPhone, the space is available for you to use.

The Cricut Maker itself is a versatile machine with interchangeable cutting and marking heads, literally a goldmine of an asset to many material cutting entrepreneurs out there. It has different versions you can use, depending on the kind of project you are working on and the set of features that best help you achieve your design goals.

Chapter 1
Materials that can be used with Cricut machines

Cricut machines have been designed to handle a wide variety of materials. Most of the devices can work with most materials, but they do have specialties among them. Read on for more information on the Cricut Explore One, Cricut Explore Air 2, Cricut Maker, and Cricut EasyPress 2 and the materials that work best with each.

Cricut Explore One

This machine only has one carriage, so you might find yourself swapping out tools more often than with the other devices. This machine can cut over 100 different materials. It can also write and score. Here's a sampling of some of the most common materials used with the Explore One

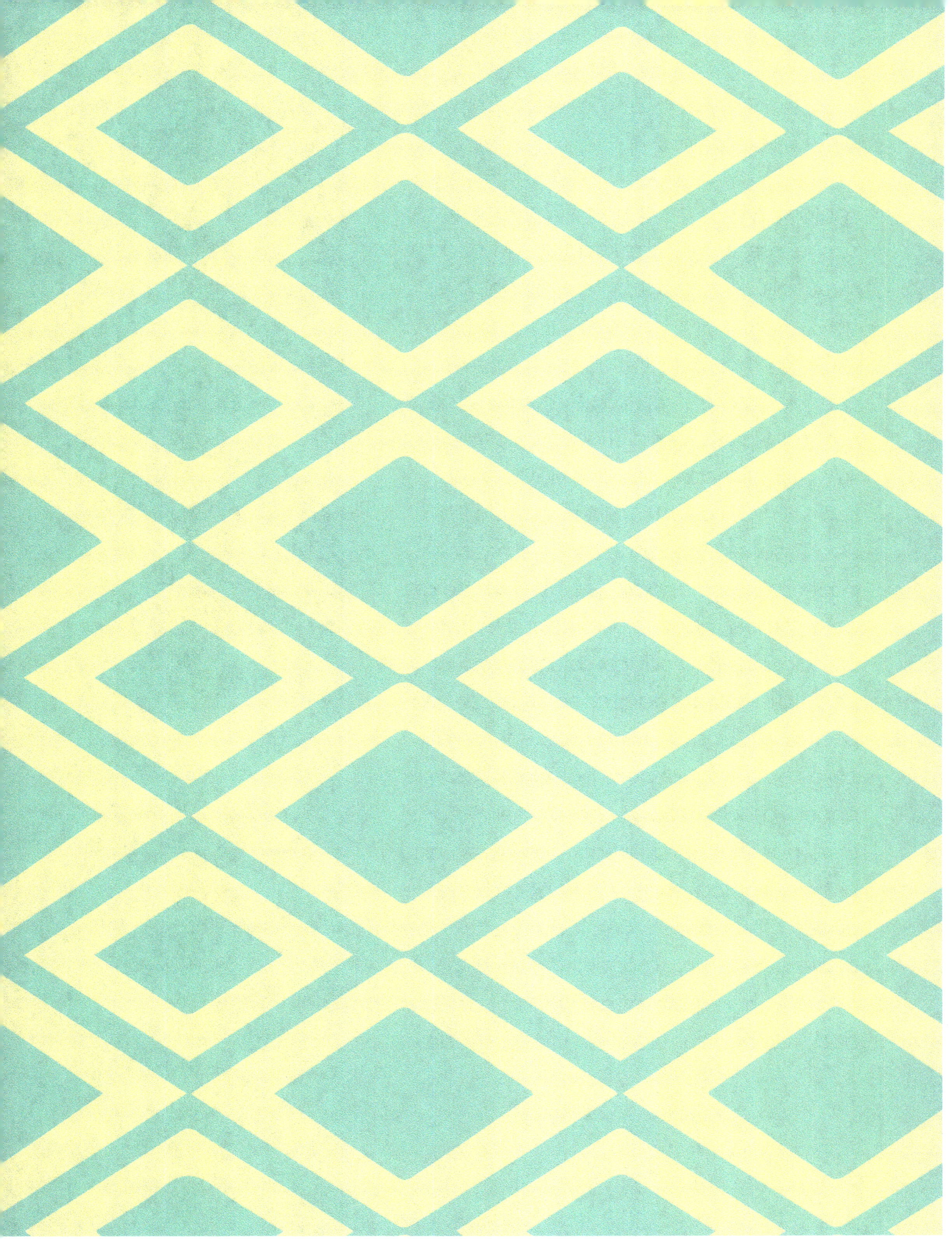

machine.

Vinyl - Vinyl, outdoor vinyl, glitter vinyl, metallic vinyl, matte vinyl, stencil vinyl, dry erase vinyl, chalkboard vinyl, adhesive foils, holographic vinyl, printable vinyl, vinyl transfer tape, iron-on vinyl, glitter iron-on vinyl, foil iron-on, holographic iron-on, printable iron-on for light or dark fabric, flocked iron-on vinyl, and neon iron-on vinyl

Paper - Cardstock, glitter cardstock, pearl paper, poster board, scrapbook paper, vellum, party foil, cereal boxes, construction paper, copy paper, flat cardboard, flocked cardstock and paper, foil embossed paper, freezer paper, kraft board, kraft paper, metallic cardstock and paper, notebook paper, paper grocery bags, parchment paper, paper board, pearl cardstock and paper, photographs, mat board, rice paper, solid core cardstock, watercolor paper, and wax paper

Fabric - Burlap, canvas, cotton, denim, duck cloth, faux leather, faux suede,

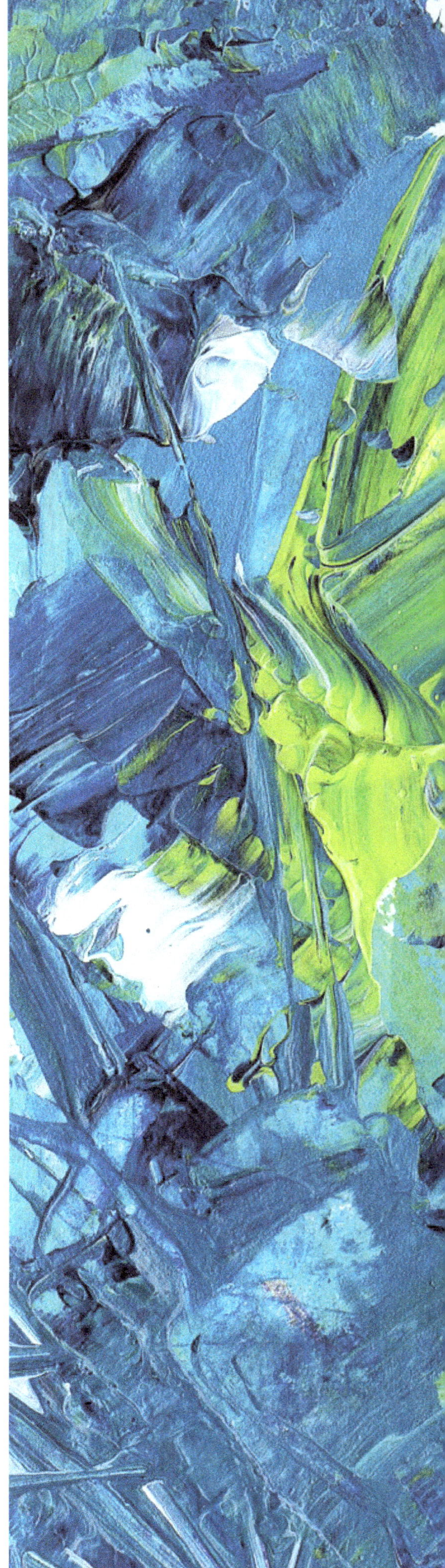

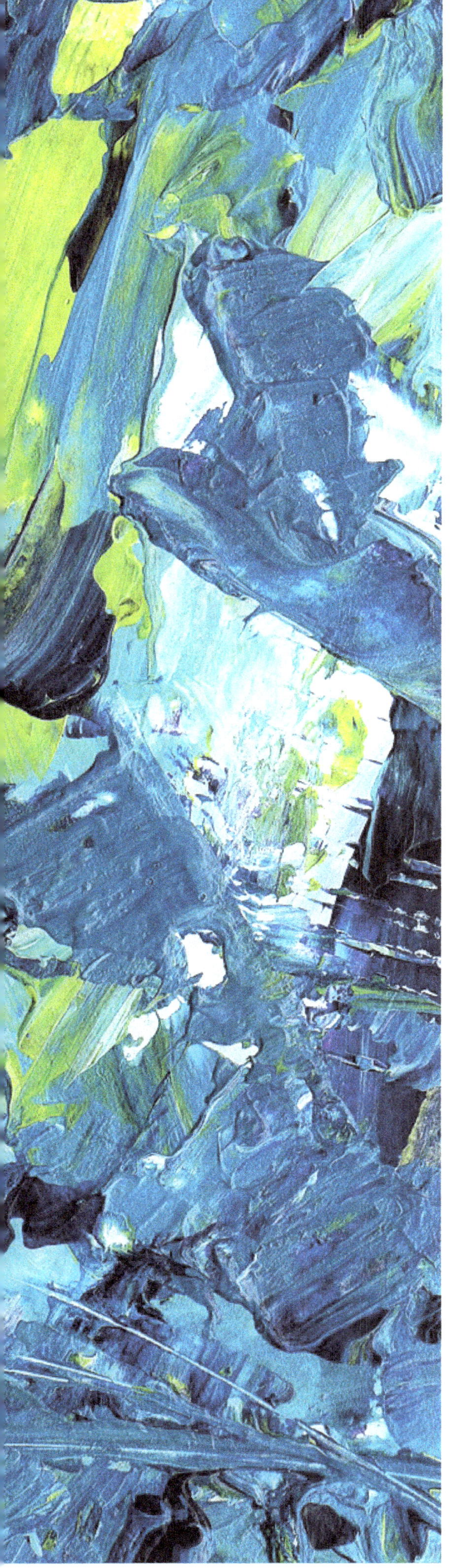

felt, flannel, leather, linen, metallic leather, oilcloth, polyester, printable fabric, silk, and wool felt

Specialty - Adhesive foil, adhesive wood, aluminum sheets, aluminum foil, balsa wood, birch wood, corkboard, corrugated paper, craft foam, duct tape, embossable foil, foil acetate, glitter foam, magnet sheets, metallic vellum, paint chips, plastic, sticker paper, shrink plastic, stencil material, tissue paper, temporary tattoo paper, transparency film, washi sheets and tape, window cling, wood veneer, and wrapping paper

Cricut Explore Air 2

The Explore Air 2 can cut the same materials as the Explore One. The difference is that it has two carriages instead of one, so it's easier to swap between tools. It's also a bit faster than the Explore One. The Air machines have wireless and Bluetooth capabilities, so you can use the Cricut

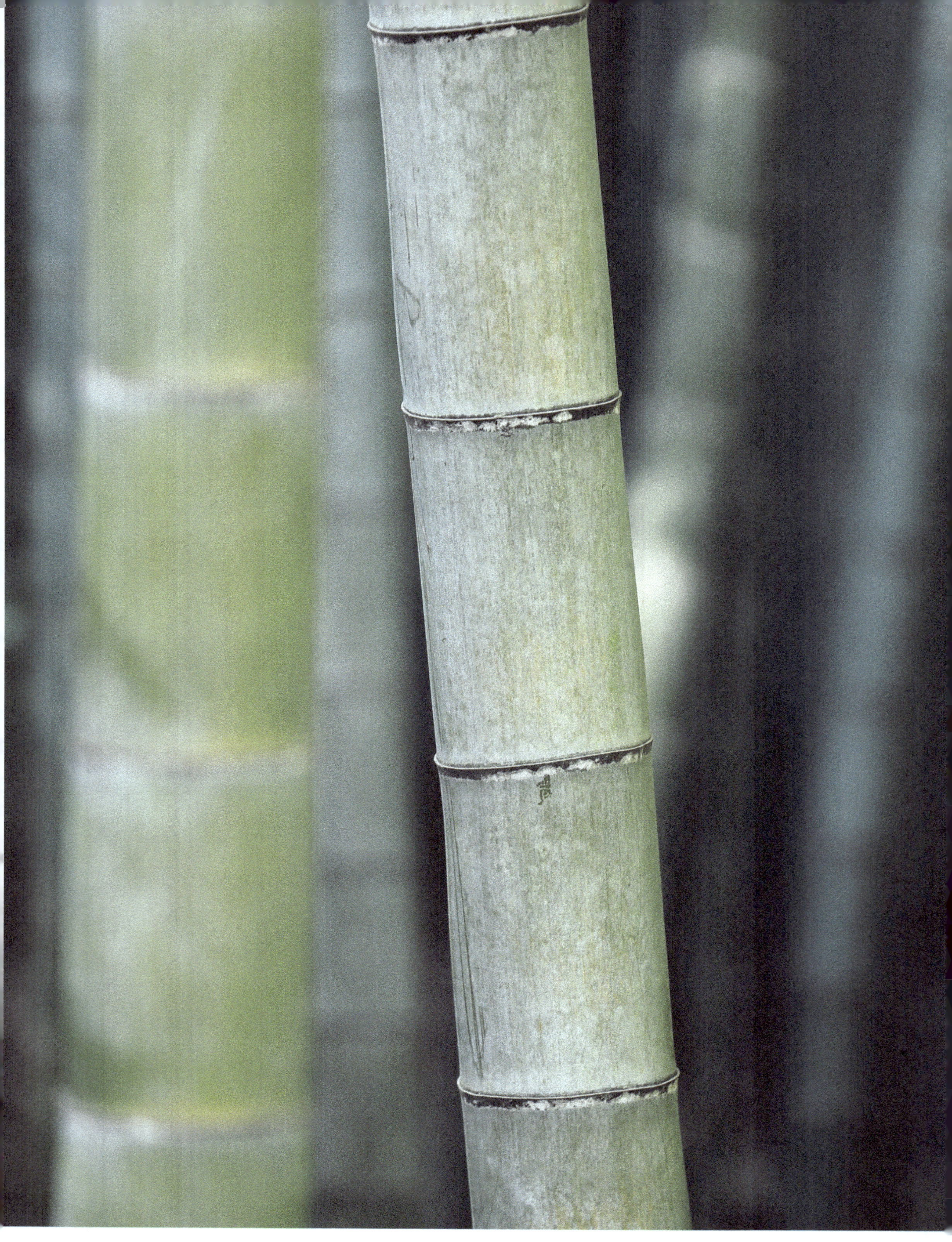

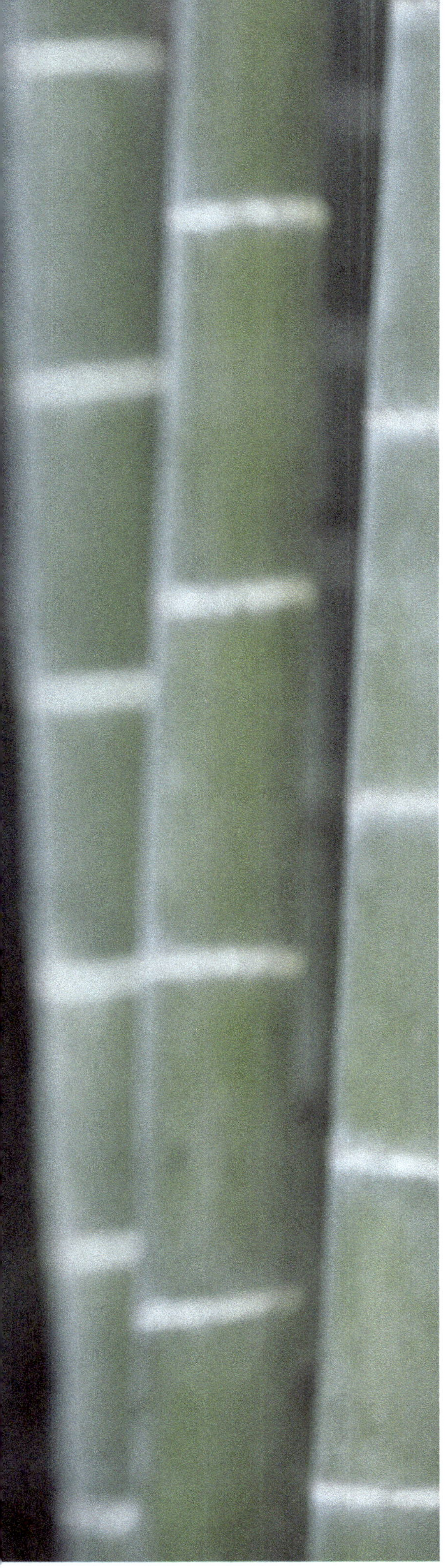

Design Space on your phone, tablet, or laptop without connecting directly to the machine.

Cricut Maker

The Cricut Maker has about 10x the cutting power of the Explore machines. It includes a rotary blade and a knife blade, so in addition to all the above materials, it can cut into more robust fabrics and materials. With the sharper edges, it's also better at cutting into more delicate materials without damaging them. Here's a list of some of the additional materials the Maker can cut.

- Acrylic felt
- Bamboo fabric
- Bengaline
- Birch
- Boucle
- Broadcloth
- Burlap

- Velvet
- Calico
- Cambric
- Canvas
- Carbon fiber
- Cashmere
- Challis
- Chambray
- Chantilly lace
- Charmeuse satin
- Chiffon
- Chintz
- Chipboard
- Corduroy
- Crepe paper
- Cutting mat protector
- Dotted Swiss
- Double cloth
- Double knit
- Dupioni silk
- EVA foam
- Eyelet
- Faille
- Fleece
- Foulard

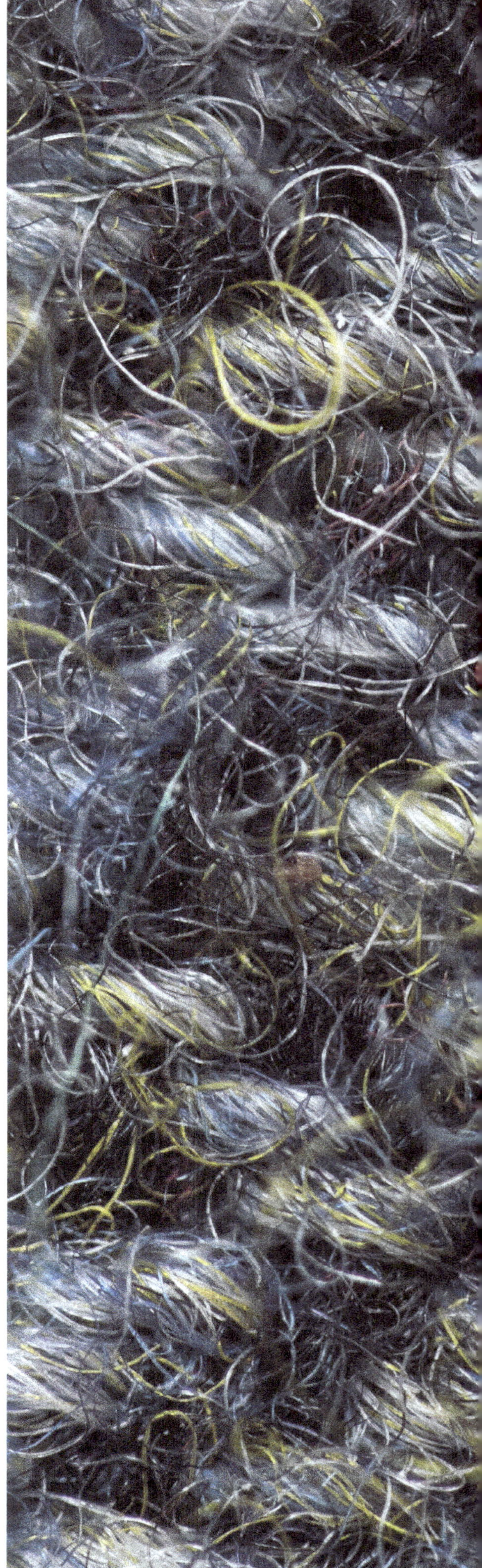

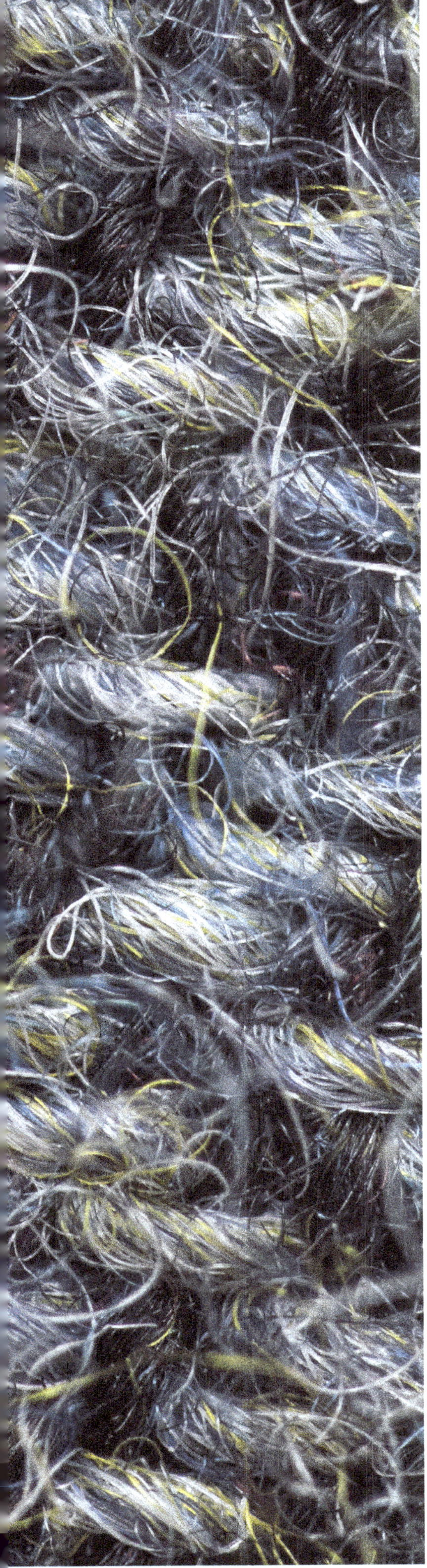

- Gabardine
- Gauze
- Gel sheet
- Georgette
- Gossamer
- Gross point
- Habutai
- Heather
- Heavy watercolor paper
- Homespun fabric
- Interlock knit
- Jacquard
- Jersey
- Jute
- Kevlar
- Bonded silk
- Tafetta
- Tulle
- Tweed
- Wool crepe

Cricut EasyPress 2

The Cricut EasyPress 2 is a small, convenient heat press. It works with any type of iron-on material and can adhere to fabrics, wood, paper, and more. Cricut also offers Infusible inks that are transferred to the material using heat. The EasyPress is an excellent alternative to iron, as it heats more quickly and more evenly.

Crafting Blanks

The objects you decorate using your Cricut can be referred to as blanks. This can be absolutely any object, and it can be something you stick vinyl to, etch, paint, draw on, write on, or anything else you can think of. They're called blanks because they provide a mostly blank surface to be decorated, though they can also have colors or designs. Some popular blanks are cups, mugs, wine or champagne glasses, travel mugs, tumblers, and other such drinking vessels. Craft stores will usually sell these, but you can find them at almost any store. They don't need to be conside-red a "craft" supply for you to use. Most stores have a selection of plain cups and mugs or travel mugs and tumblers with no designs. As long as you can

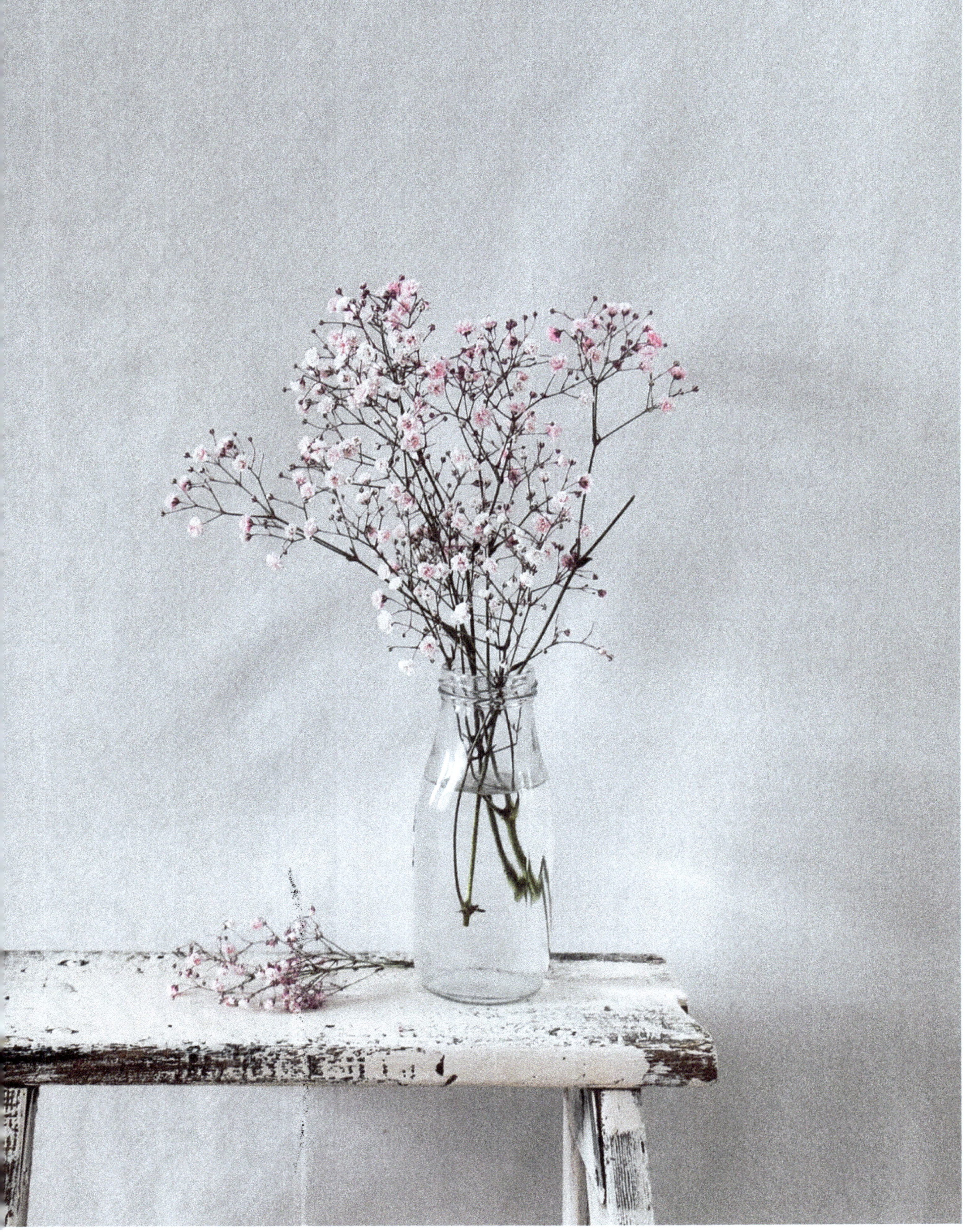

imagine a Cricut project with it, it's fair game.

Drink wares aren't the only kitchen or dining-related blanks. Get creative with plates, bowls, and serving utensils. Find blank placemats or coasters at most stores. Decorate mason or other types of jars. Dry goods containers, measuring cups, food storage containers, pitchers, and jugs-anything you can put in your kitchen can serve as an excellent blank for your projects.

Clothing is another popular choice for Cricut projects. T-shirts are easy to make with iron-on vinyl, and you can find cheap blanks at any store or a more extensive selection at craft sto-res. Craft stores will typically have a large selection of clothing blanks, such as t-shirts, long sleeve shirts, ball caps, plain white shoes, plain bags, and so on. Thrift stores or consignment shops can be an unusual option as well. You could find a shirt with an interesting pattern that you'd like to add an iron-

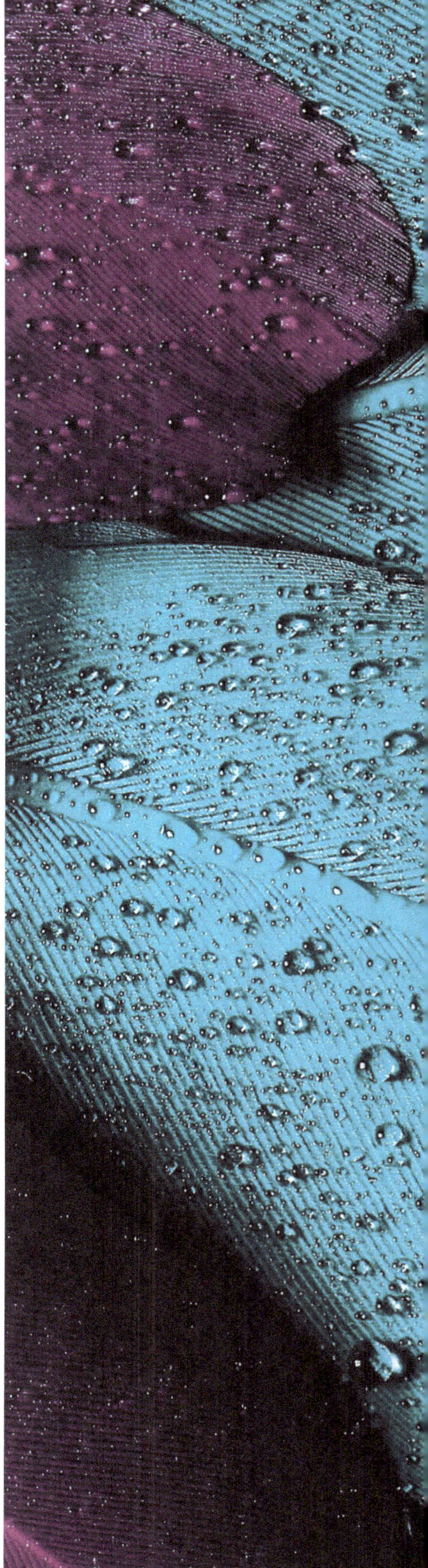

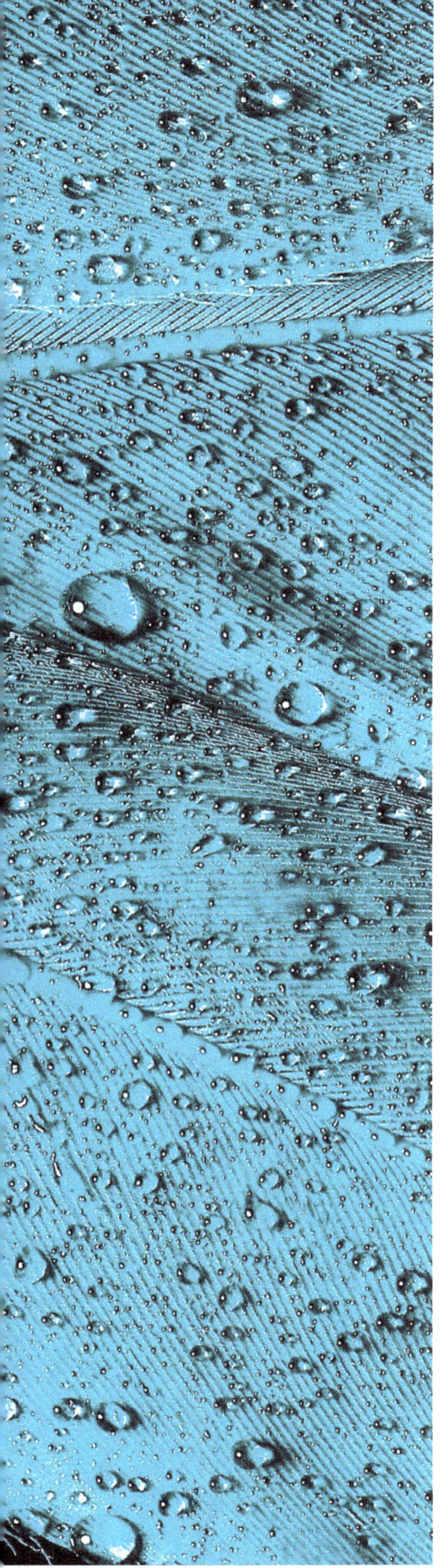

on to something similar.

Glass is fun to work with and has many project options with your Cricut machine. Glass blocks can be found at craft or hardware stores. Many stores that carry kitchenware will have plain glass cutting boards, or you can find them online. Craft stores and home goods stores could sell glass trinkets or décor that you can decorate. You can even buy full panes of glass at your local hardware store and have them cut it to your desired size.

There are plenty of blanks related to electronics, as well. Electronics stores, online stores, and some craft stores offer phone and tablet case blanks. They might be clear, white or black, or colored. Portable battery packs are another option as well. These blanks are often significantly cheaper than already decorated ones, or you can buy them in bulk for a lower price. Get your phone case for a lower price and customize it how you like.

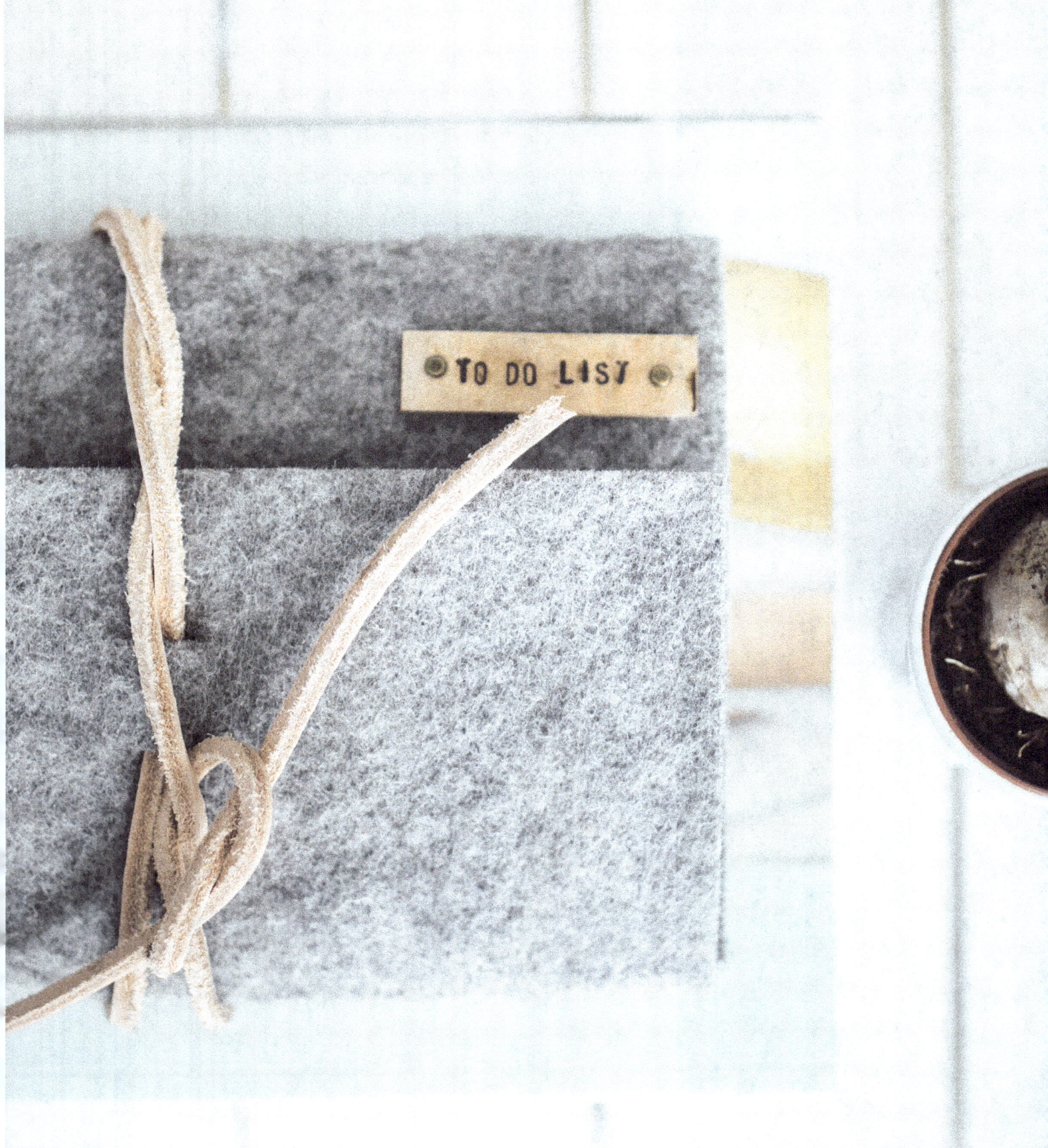
TO DO LIST

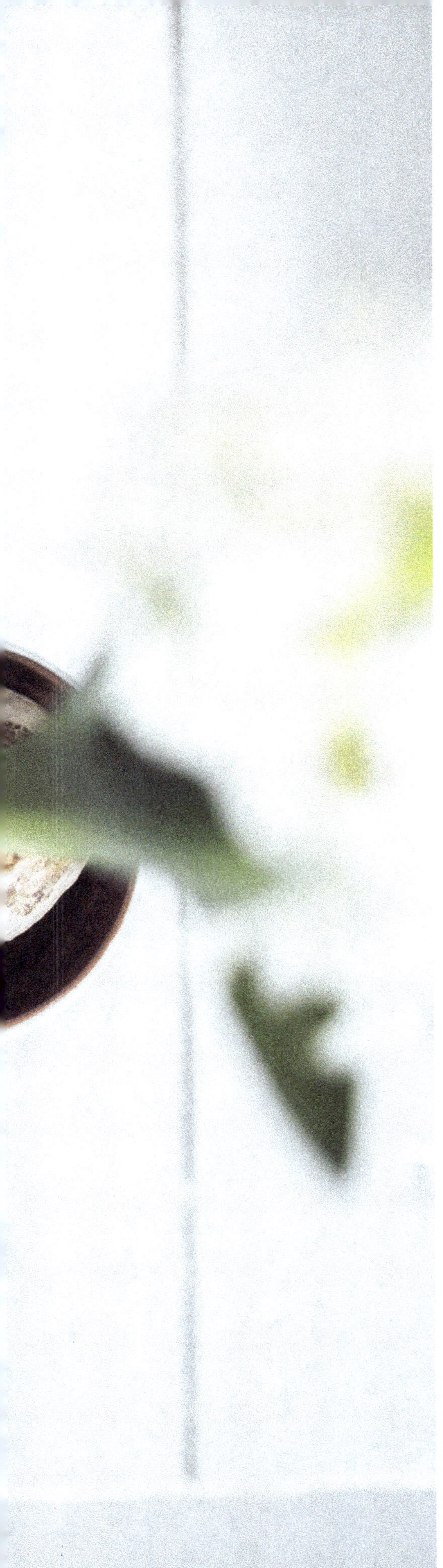

Book covers make great blanks, as well. Customize the surface of a sketchbook, notebook, or journal. Repair an aged book. Or, create a new book cover for a plain one that you have. If you have old books that you aren't going to read, create a new fake cover for them and use them as décor.

Felt

Blended fibers between natural and synthetic are also standard among craft felts. Felt is commonly used to help young children distinguish among different types of textiles. Felt is also widely used in craft projects for all ages. The felt is easily cut with your Cricut Machine; no Deep Cut blade required! Felt can be used for fun décor, kid's crafts, baby toys, stuffed shapes, and more! When starting on the Cricut Maker, this is one of the best materials, to begin with. This material is very forgiving and will allow you to keep the gift-giving spirit going! This material is also great for creating faux flowers. You can bring the outside in without the maintenance or worrying about children or pets getting into a mess!

How to use materials for Cricut machine

With Cricut, the projects' ideas are so vast; you'll be amazed at how much you can do. So, what are some ideas that could work for you? Here are a few that you can consider and some of the best project ideas for those stumped on where to begin!

Easy Projects

CUSTOM SHIRTS

Custom shirts are straightforward. You would like to use the iron-on vinyl because it's easy to work with. Just take your image and upload it into Design

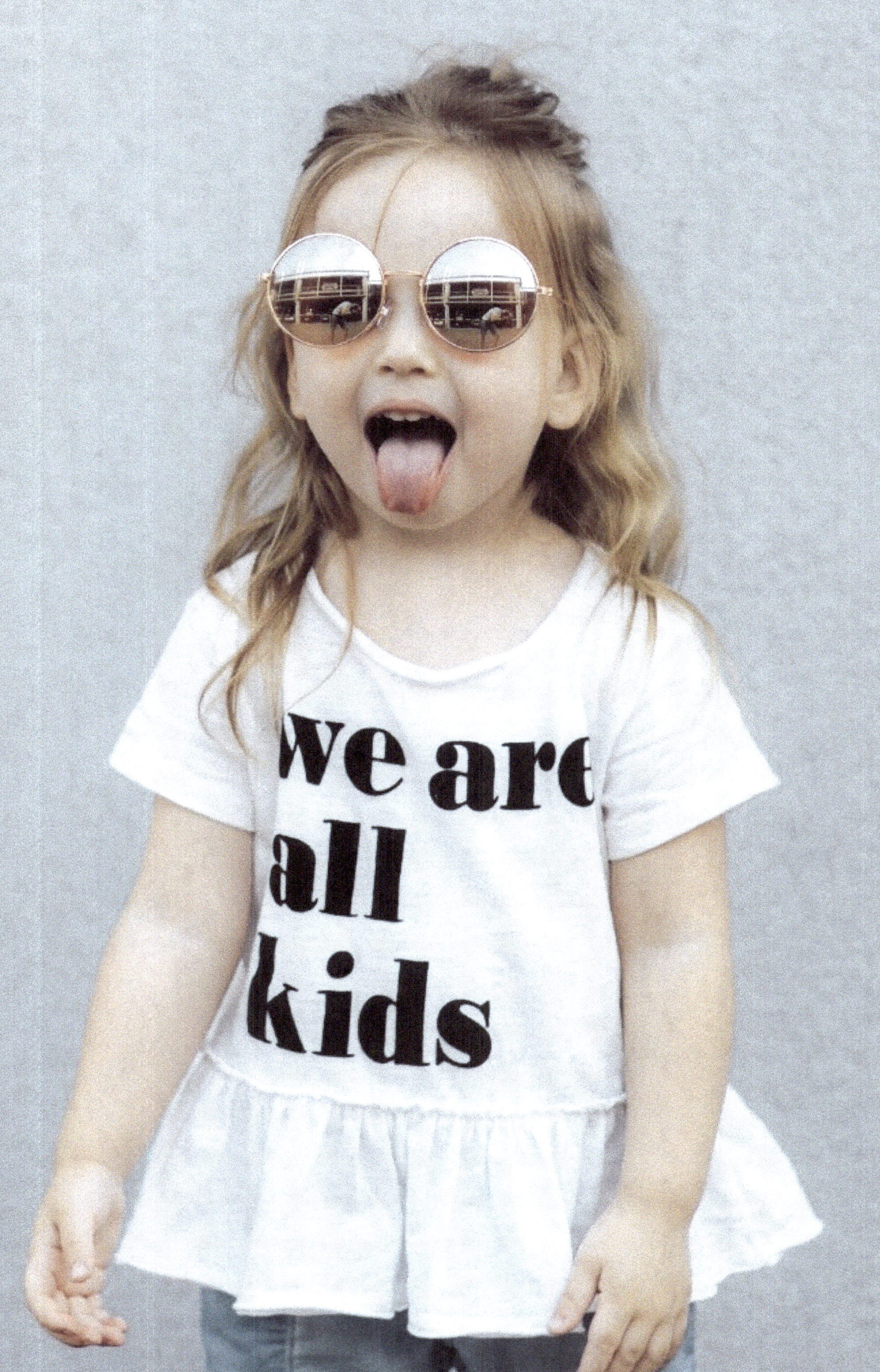
we are
all
kids

Space. Then, go to the canvas and find the image you want. Once you've selected the image, you click on the whitespace that will be cut - remember to get the insides, too. Ensure that you choose a cut image, not print from the cut image, and then place it on the canvas to your liking size. Put the iron-on vinyl shiny side down, turn it on, and select iron-on from the menu. Choose to cut, and make sure you mirror the image. Once done, pull off the extra vinyl to remove the vinyl between the letters. There you go! A simple shirt.

VINYL DECALS

Vinyl can also be used to make personalized items, such as water bottle decals. First, design the text - you can pretty much use whatever you want for this. From here, create a second box and make an initial or whatever design you want. Make sure that you resize this to fit the water bottle, as well. From here, load your vinyl, and make

sure that you use transfer tape on the vinyl itself once you cut it out. Finally, when you adhere the lettering to the bottle, go from the center and then push outwards, smoothing as you go. It takes a bit, but there you have it - simple water bottles that children will love! This is a beautiful, simple project for those of us who aren't really that artistically inclined but want to get used to making Cricut items.

PRINTABLE STICKERS

Printable stickers are the next project. This is super simple and fun for parents and kids. The Explore Air 2 machine works best.

With this one, you want the print then cut feature since it makes it much more comfortable. To begin, go to Design Space and download images of ice cream or whatever you want, or upload pictures of your own. You click on a new project, and on the left side that says images, you can choose the ones you like and insert more of these on there.

From here, choose the image and flatten it since this will make it into one piece rather than just a separate file for each. Resize as needed to make sure that they fit where you're putting them.

You can copy/paste each element until you're done. Once ready, press saves and then chooses this as a print, then cut the image. Click the big button at the bottom that says make it. Make sure everything is right, then press continues, and from there, you can load the sticker paper into the machine. Make sure to adjust this to the right setting, which for sticker paper is the vinyl set. Put the form into there and load them in, and when ready, the press goes - it will then cut the stickers as needed.

From there, take them out and decorate. You can use ice cream or whatever sticker image you want!

PERSONALIZED PILLOWS

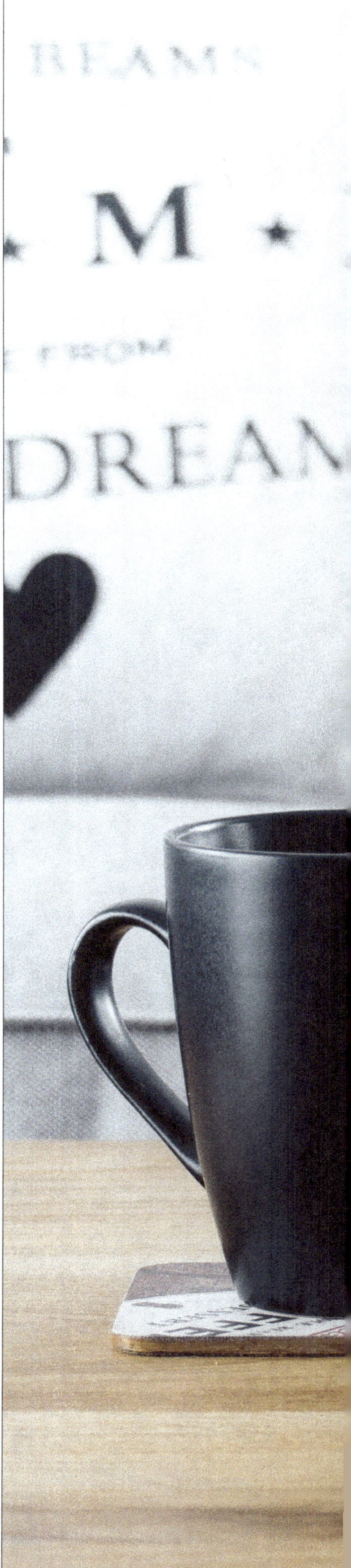

Love, LAUGH
& HAPPIL
Ever After

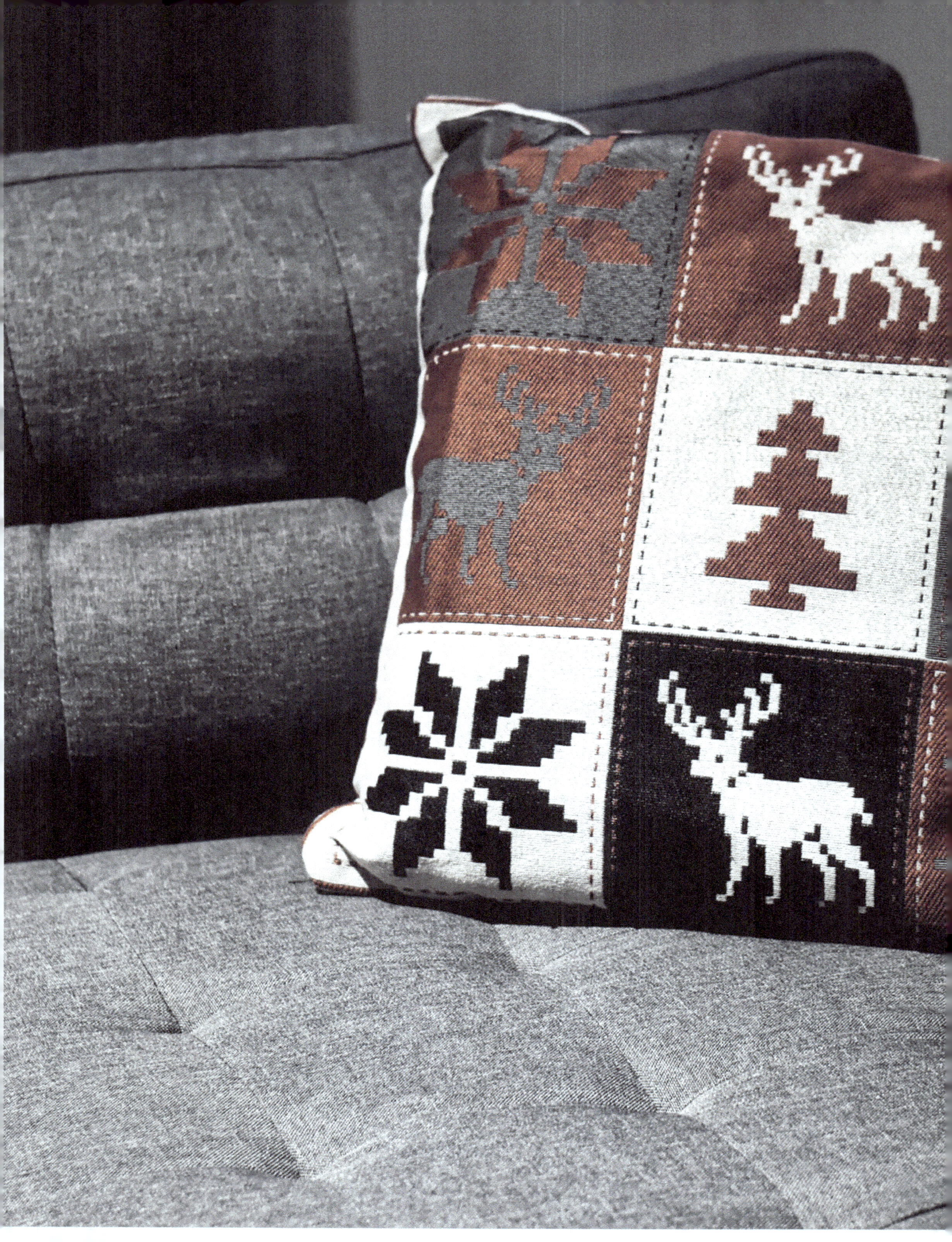

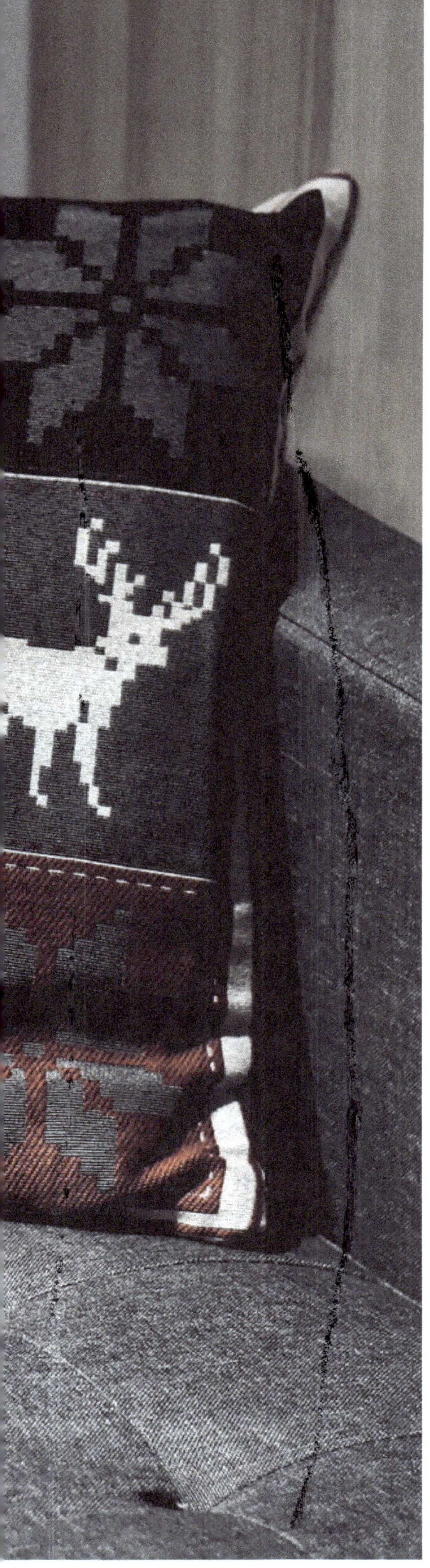

Personalized pillows are another fun idea and are incredibly easy to make. To begin, you open up Design Space and choose a new project. From here, select the icon at the bottom of the screen itself, choosing your font. Type the words you want, and drag the text as needed to make it bigger.

You can also upload images, too, if you want to create a massive picture on the pillow itself.

From here, you want to press the atta-ch button for each box, so they work together, and both are figured when centered, as well.

You then press it - and you want to turn to mirror on, since this will, again, be on iron-on vinyl. From here, you load the iron-on vinyl with the shiny side down, the press continues, follow the prompts, and make sure it's not jam-med in, either.

Let the machine work its magic with cutting, and from there, you can press the weeding tool to get the middle areas out.

Set your temperature on the easy press for the right settings, then push it onto the material, ironing it on and letting it sit for 10 to 15 seconds. Let it cool, and then take the transfer sheet off.

There you have it! A simple pillow that works wonders for your crafting needs.

CARDS!

Finally, cards are a great project idea for Cricut makers. They're simple, and you can do the entire project with cardstock.

To make this, you first want to open up Design Space, and from there, put your design in. If you like images of ice cream, then use that. If you want to make Christmas cards, you can do that, too. You can design whatever you want on this.

Now, you'll then want to add the text. You can choose the font you want to use, and from there, write out the message on the card, such as "Merry Christmas." At this point, instead of choo-

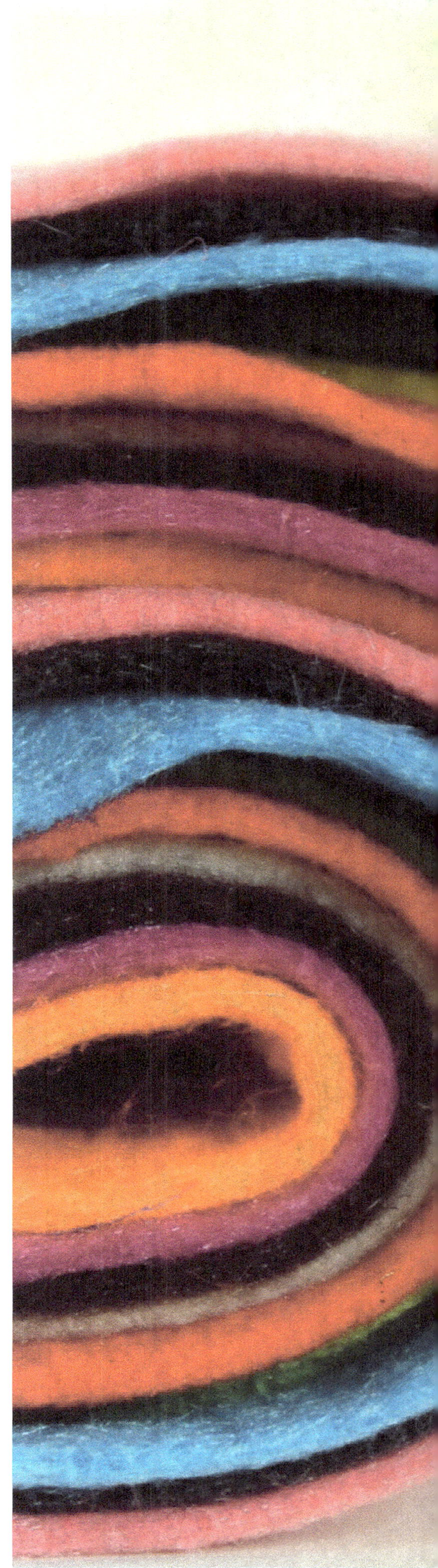

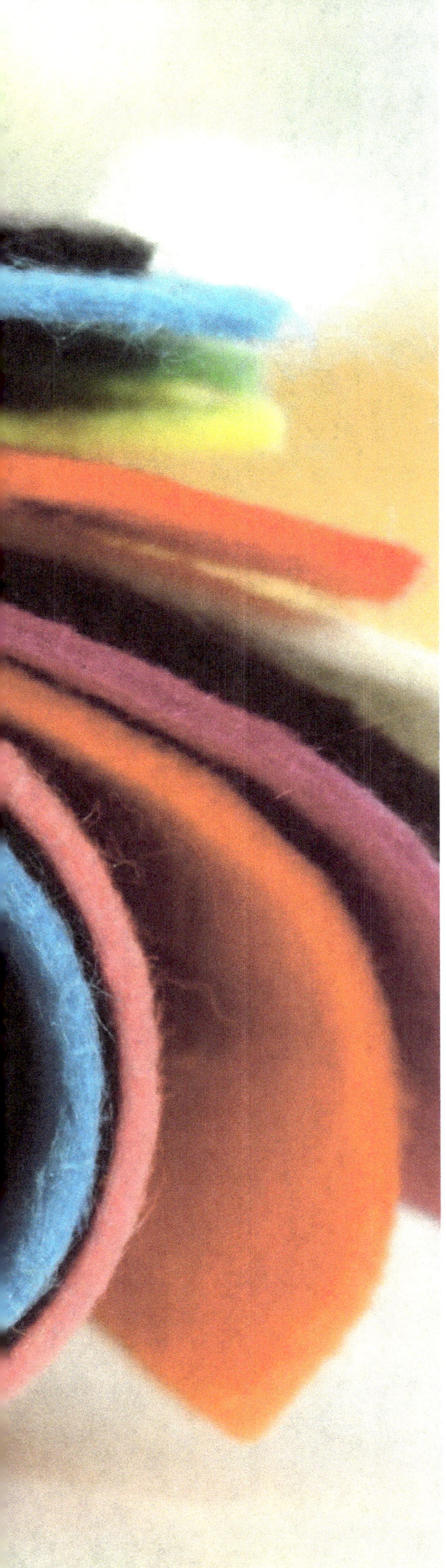

sing to cut, you want to select the right option - the make it option. You don't have to mirror this but check that your design fits appropriately on the cardstock itself. When choosing material for writing, make sure you select the cardstock. From there, insert your cardstock into the machine, and then, when ready, you can press go, and the Cricut machine will design your card. This may take a minute, but once it's done, you'll have an excellent card in place. It's super easy to use.

Cricut cards are a great personalized way to express yourself, creating a one-of-a-kind, sentimental piece for you to gift to friends and family.

Medium Projects

CRICUT CAKE TOPPERS

Cricut cake toppers have a little bit of added difficulty because they require some precise scoring. The Cricut maker is probably the best piece of equipment for the job, and here, we'll tell you how

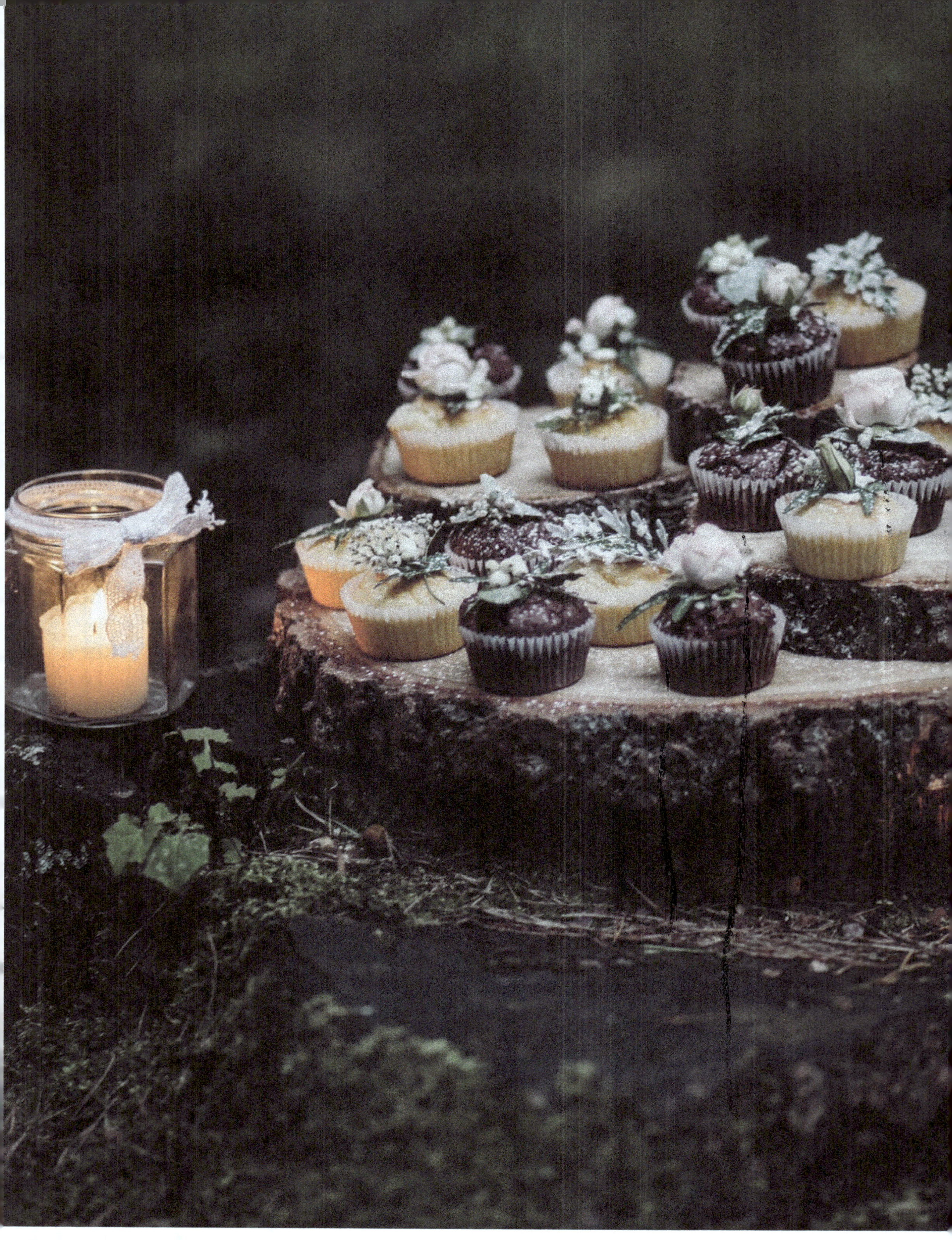

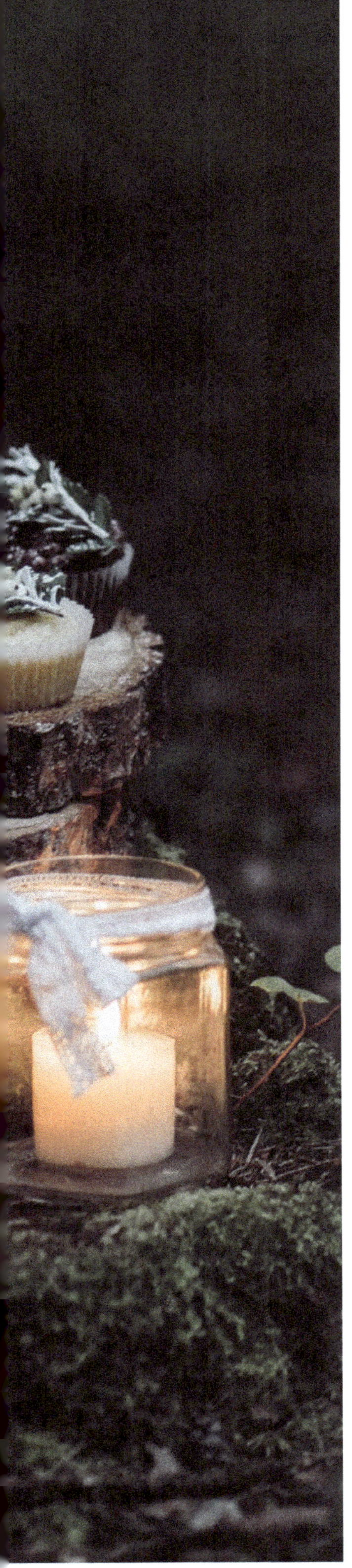

to do it. The scoring tool is your best bet since this will make different shapes even more comfortable. You will want to make sure you have cardstock and the cutting mat, along with a fine-point blade for cutting. The tape is also handy for these.

First, go to Design Space and choose the rosettes you want. From there, the press makes it and follows the prompts. The single wheel will make one crease, and the double wheel will make a parallel wheel that will crease - perfect for specialty items. Plus, the dual wheel is thicker, so it's easier to fold.

Once you score everything, you remove it and replace the scoring wheel with the fine-point blade.

From here, you simply fold everything and just follow the line. This should make the rosette, and you can then use contrasting centers and create many of these to form a lovely backdrop.

CRICUT GIFT BAGS

Remember to put the foil poster board face-down on the mat itself to help prevent the material from cracking and showing through to the white backdrop when you fold them together after you score them. To make these, you want to implement the template you'd like to use in Design Space. From here, you do suggest cutting out the initial design first and then putting it back in to create scoring lines, following the same steps. After that, you can then take your item, fold it along the score lines, and then use adhesive or glue to help put it all together. This is a great personalized way to do it but can be complicated to work with at first.

CRICUT FABRIC COASTERS

Fabric coasters with a Cricut maker are great, and they need only a few supplies. These include the maker itself, cotton fabric, fusible fleece, a rotary cutting mat or some scissors, a sewing machine, and an iron.

Cut the fabric to about 12 inches to fit the cutting mat - if it's longer, you can hang it off; be careful.

From here, go to Design Space, then click shapes and make a heart. You can do this with other conditions, too. Resize

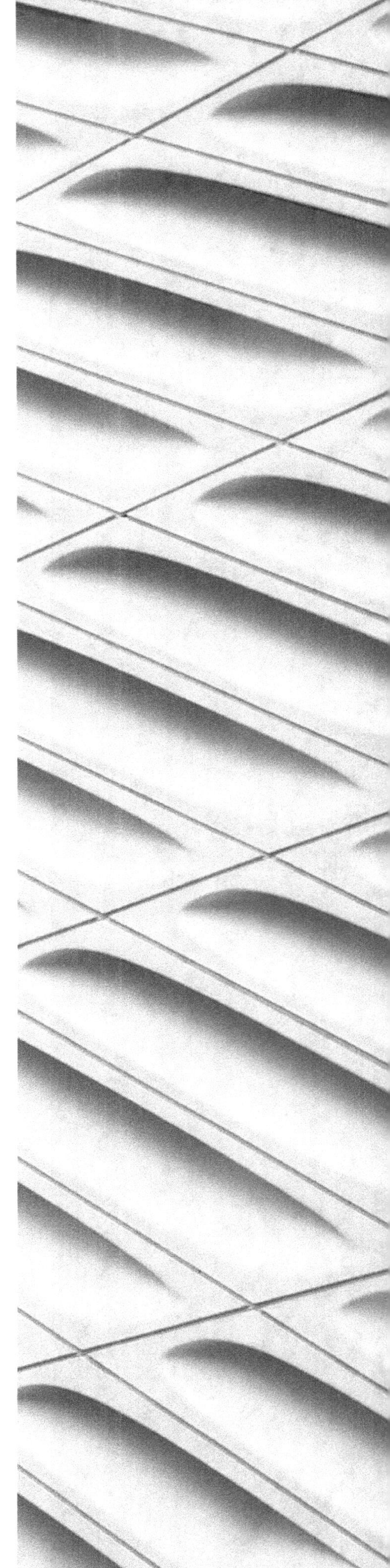

it to about 5 inches wide. Press makes it, and you'll want to make sure you create four copies. Press continue, and then choose medium fabrics similar to cotton. You then load the mat and cut, and then you do it again with the fusible fleece on the cutting mat, changing it to 4.75 inches. This time, when choosing the material, go to more and then select fusible fleece. Cut the fusible fleece, and then attach these to the heart's back with the iron and repeat with the second.

Clip the curves, turn it inside out, and then fold in the edges and stitch it.

There you go - a fusible fleece heart coaster. It's a little bit more complicated, but it's worth trying out.

Difficult Projects

GIANT VINYL STENCILS

Vinyl stencils are a good thing to create, too, but they can be challenging. Big vinyl stencils make for an excellent Cricut project, and you can use them in various places, including bedrooms for kids.

You only need the explore Air 2, the vinyl

that works for it, a pallet, sander, and, of course, paint and brushes. The first step is preparing the pallet for painting or whatever surface you plan on using this for.

From here, you create the mermaid tail (or any other large image) in Design Space. Now, you'll learn immediately that big pieces are hard to cut and impossible to do all at once in Design Space.

What you do is a section of each design accordingly and removes any middle pieces. You can add square shapes to the image, slicing it into pieces to be cut on a cutting mat that fits.

At this point, you cut out the design by pressing make it, choosing your material, and working in sections.

From here, you put it on the surface that you're using, piecing this together with each line, and you should have one image after piecing it all together. Then, draw out the line on vinyl and then paint the initial design. For the second set of stencils, you can simply trace the first one and then paint the inside of them. At this point, you should have the design finished. When done, remo-

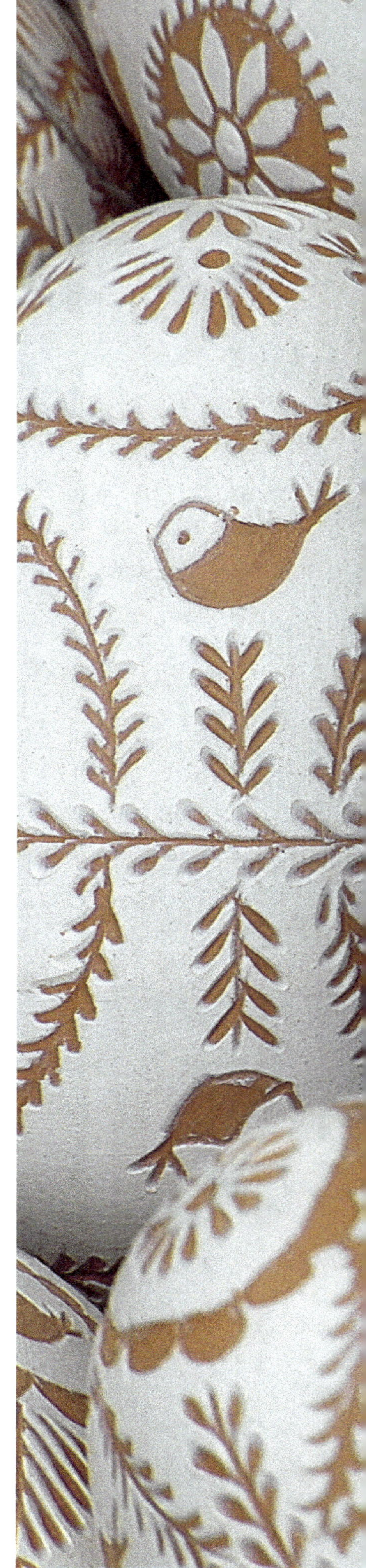

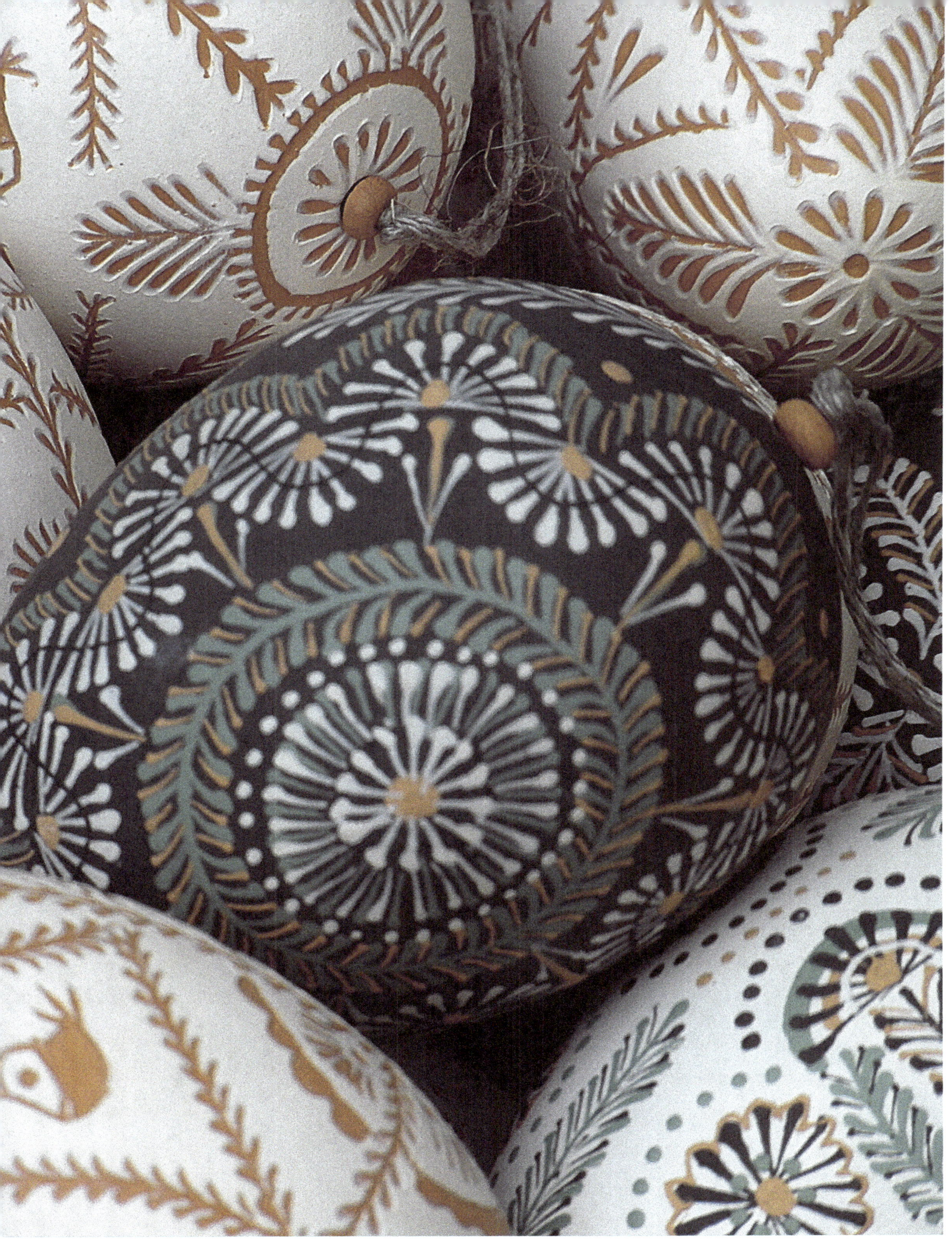

ve it very carefully.

And there you have it! More oversized stencils can be a bit of a project since it involves trying to use multiple designs all at once. Still, with the right care and suitable designs, you'll be able to create whatever it is you need to in Design Space so you can get the results you're looking for.

Where Do You Find Material?

One of Cricut Design Space's exciting parts is that the materials are not hard to find; they are all around you. There are online stores where you can quickly get the materials you want. Although different e-stores have varying prices, the point is to get the ideal quality. There are four popular online stores where Cricut machine users, both beginners, and professionals, get materials for their Cricut projects, and they are; Cricut.com, Amazon, Joann, and Michaels. These stores provide almost every supply

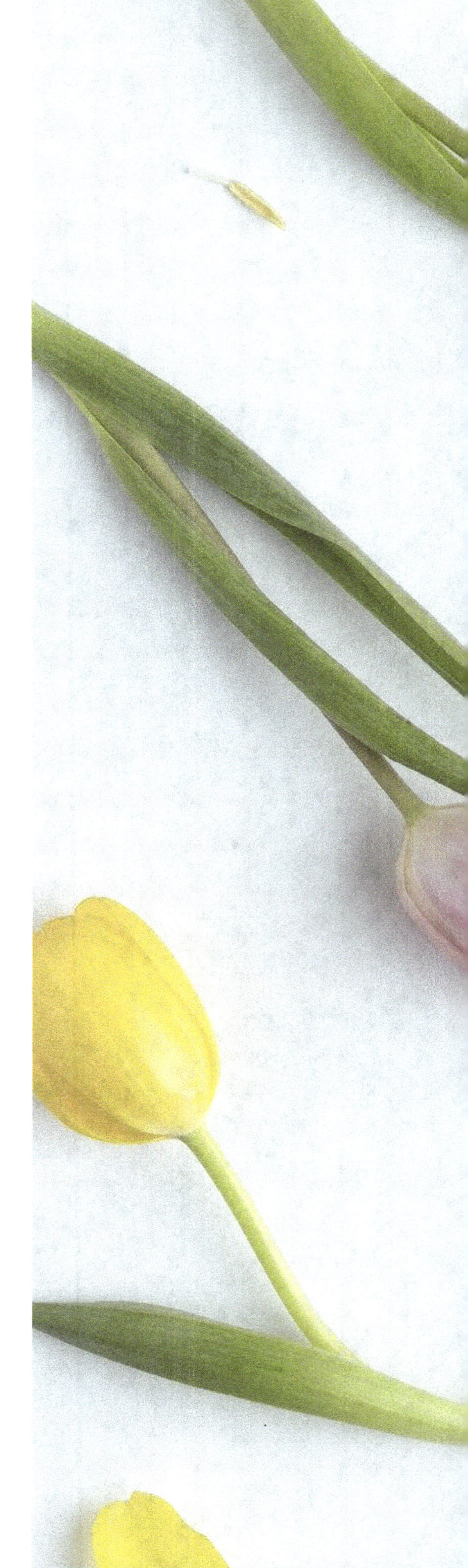

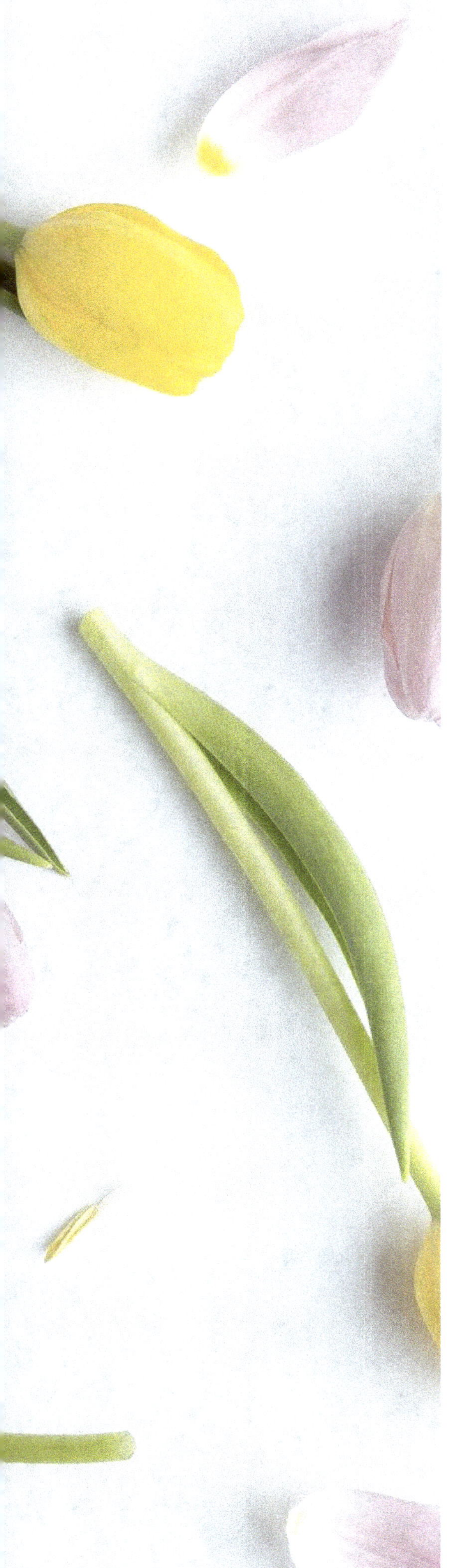

and bundle you'll be needing. They have the materials, tools, and accessories, and even the Cricut machines required. Feel free to visit each store and compare their prices before purchasing.

Also, you can look around for stores in your local area where sell the most common types of materials that can be used on Cricut machines, mostly paper products.

At this stage, we have covered most of the basics of Cricut machines, materials, tools, and accessories. You should now know their functionalities and purposes to some extent. It's high time we proceeded to the technical and tricky part of making use of Cricut for different designs and crafts. We will not discuss much the properties of Cricut machines, materials, tools, or accessories from here onward. It will be majorly about how you can set up your Cricut machine and what you can do with it. We're getting to the exciting parts.

If you need to upgrade your Cricut machines, buy any material, tool or ac-

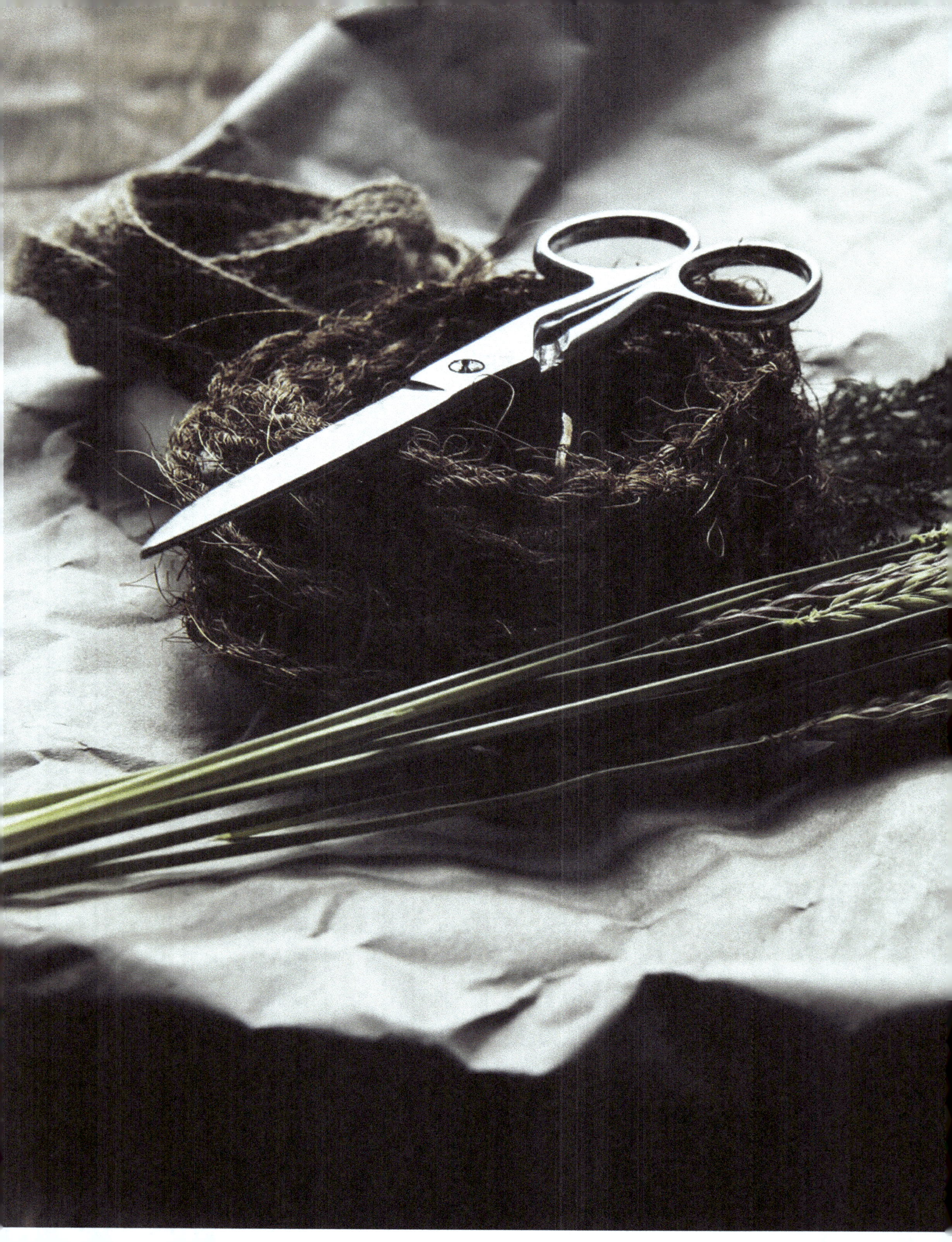

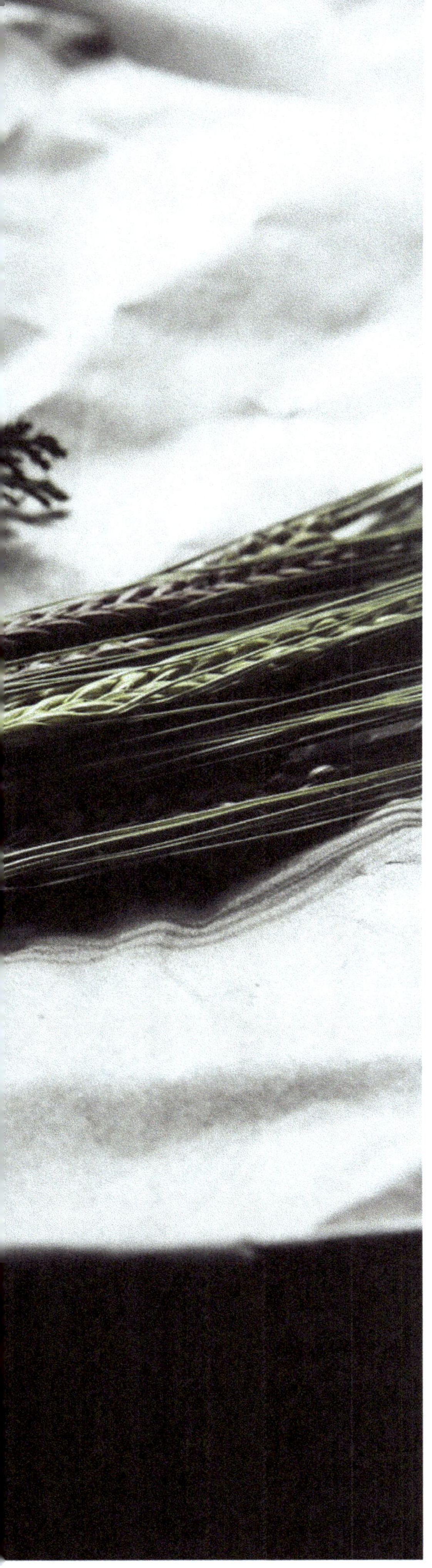

cessory, you should make plans for that now. The more resources you have, the more you can explore.

How to cut materials with the Cricut machine

There are many materials a Cricut can cut. Vinyl is one of the most popular items people like to use. There is also a wide range of vinyl types; Cricut claims there are over 100 types of materials the machine can cut. Some of the top materials include:

- Iron-on
- Paper
- Vinyl
- Fabric

PLASTIC

Other items include crafting materials, like foam, paper with glitter, Washi tape, thick materials like woods, leather, and magnets. Repurposed materials are another option and are a cheap and environmentally friendly option. Some of the things people have used include aluminum from cans, cardboard from cereal boxes, and chipboard.

TESTING CUTS

When beginning a project, always do a test cut on a scrap of material. Do not use the final material, which is often more expensive if there is a problem with the design. Try to choose a scrap material similar in weight and texture to your final material for accuracy.
Many people skip this step but end up regretting it when the material is ruined. Problems can include the cutting pressure is too hard and slices the mat, destroying the cutting mat, or at the very least, an extra cut may be required for success.
This process shouldn't take a long time, but it can save a lot of time and money afterward if a design mistake has been made.

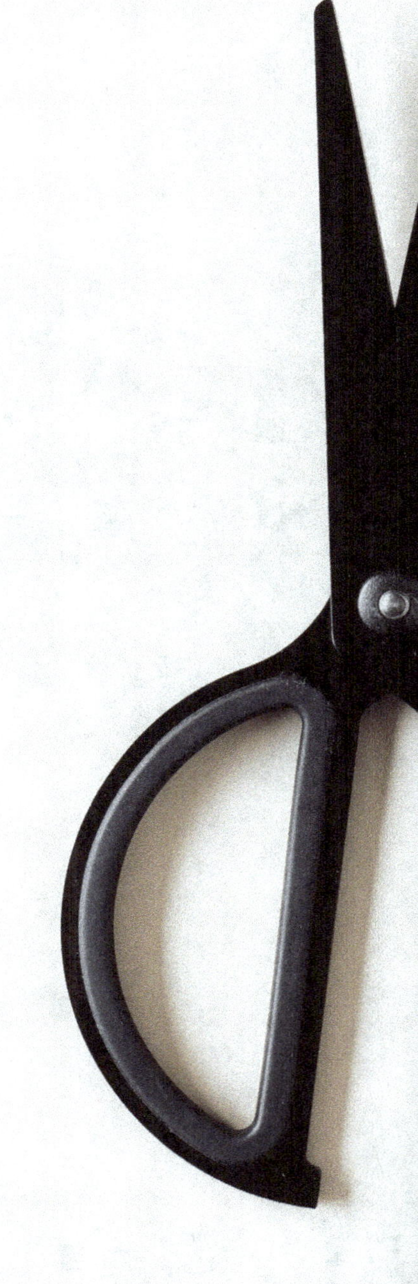

CUTTING WITH FABRICS

Fabric is a challenging medium to cut on for most Cricut machines, mainly because there are so many types of fabric to choose from. This material usually requires much trial and error to discover what works best. Sometimes a material will cut fine, while other times, it will snag and drag over the cutting mat.

A tip for working with fragile fabric fabrics is to use a bonding material, so the fabric sticks to the cutting mat. Use a roller or brayer to adhere to the mat.

If bonding is not an option, at least use stiff interfacing to help. Again, test cuts are essential in all projects, but they are significant when working with fabrics.

CUTTING WITH VINYL

After preparing and reviewing a project to be cut, when it is sent to the machine for cutting, make sure to adjust the machine's Smart Dial to the appropriate materials, for example, vinyl. Older devices may not have this material listed, and it is best to review tutorials online for suggestions on how to modify an older machine to work with this material. If working with iron-on vinyl, turn the "Mirror" switch on to ensure it prints correctly.

Select the mat that the vinyl will cut on and adhere the vinyl to the mat, placing the paper located on the back of the vinyl facing down on the mat and put it in the machine to be cut.

If there are multiple colors or vinyl to be cut, gently peel the finished, cut vinyl from the mat, and adhere to the next piece. Weeding may be required for the background vinyl before attaching it to the project.

Transfer Tape

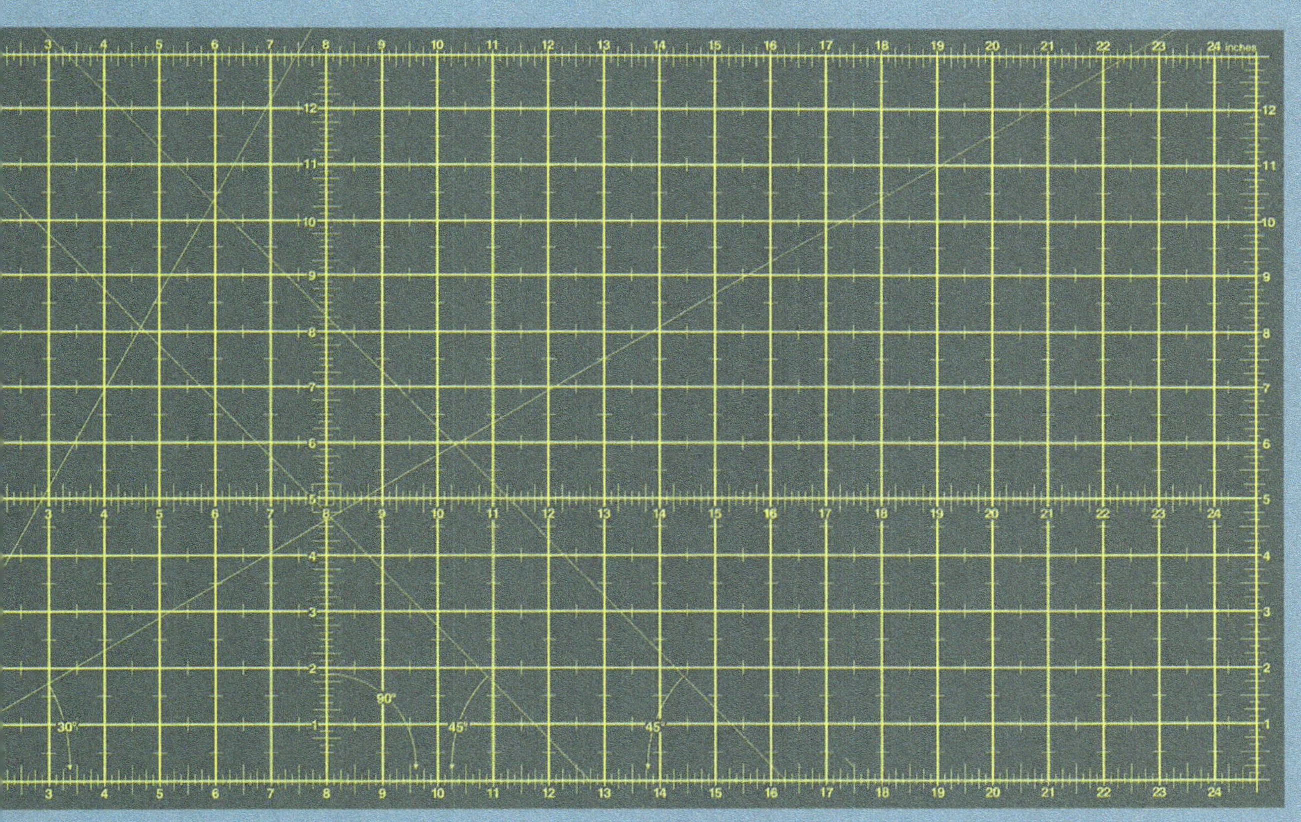

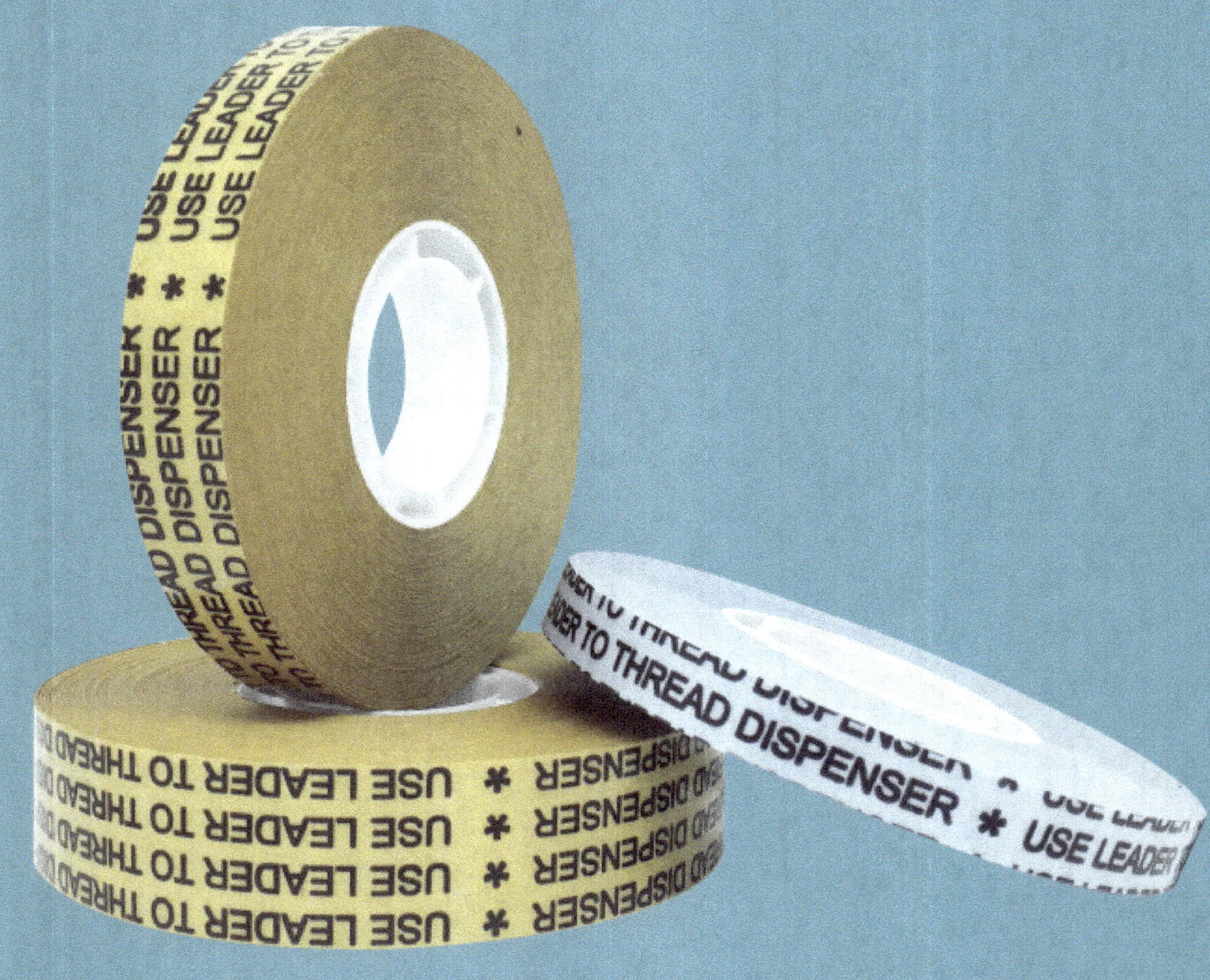
USE LEADER TO THREAD DISPENSER
USE LEADER TO THREAD DISPENSER

It is a clear, medium-strength adhesive tape that comes in sheets. You can cut pieces to your liking and use them multiple times before disposing of them. Cricut sheets are currently $8.99 at a local crafting retailer, while other brands offer a 12" roll of six to ten feet for a similar price.

While transfer tape is an integral part of the process of using your Cricut machine, the brand is not nearly as important. Do some shopping around, find a sample size that works for you and your price point, and get started!

Like with any new type of crafting project, it will take some time to get used to the supplies and products and find the things that work the best.

Now that a lot says about different materials used on Cricut machines, you should be inspired to try new projects with these materials. However, only a beginner would stop here. We're not even close to unfolding the fantastic parts of the usage of Cricut machines.

Vinyl: Professionals use vinyl materials a lot because they find them very useful and outstanding for making graphics, stencils, decals, signs, etc. There are about 11 materials made from vinyl that uses on Cricut machines.

Iron-On: This is also a vinyl product, but with a different framework. Some people know it as heat transfer vinyl. You can use this type of vinyl to design and decorate tote bags, t-shirts, caps, and other clothing items. There are around nine iron-on materials that are usable on Cricut machines.

Iron-on vinyl is also one of the treasured materials to cut with Cricut Explore Air 2. You can use the iron-on vinyl to design bags, t-shirts, and any other items.

Types of Iron-on:

- Printable iron-on

- Glossy iron-on

- Metallic iron-on

- Foil iron-on

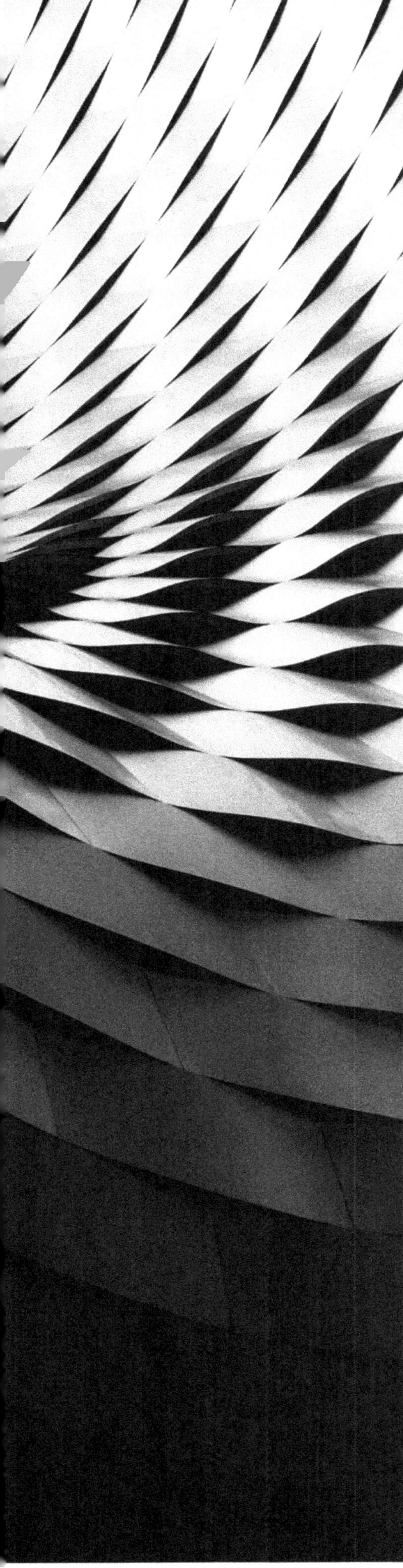

Fabric and Textiles: Fabrics are naturals on Cricut machines; they work seamlessly on almost every Cricut machine model.

Textile or Fabric is not an unusual material for some Cricut users. Still, because the variety of Fabrics available to choose from is complete, it needs to be mentioned again because some techniques and materials are a little more unusual. For example, cutting a lace-like pattern into fabrics can immediately add a color-palette of fancy lace to any project. It also makes it possible to have the same lace pattern on various complementary materials or colors.

There is a fabric blade specific to the fabric material; all you need to do is keep the Fabric set in place on the settings dial. Cricut has some fabric materials online that you can cut.

Types of Fabric:

- Leather
- Canvas
- Duck cloth
- Silk
- Linen

Infusible Ink: is an exciting material from

Cricut, allowing heat transfer on white and light-colored fabrics. It comes in different colors, patterns, and gradients, and designs to be resistant to peeling, flaking, and washing. It uses for shirts, totes, coasters, etc.

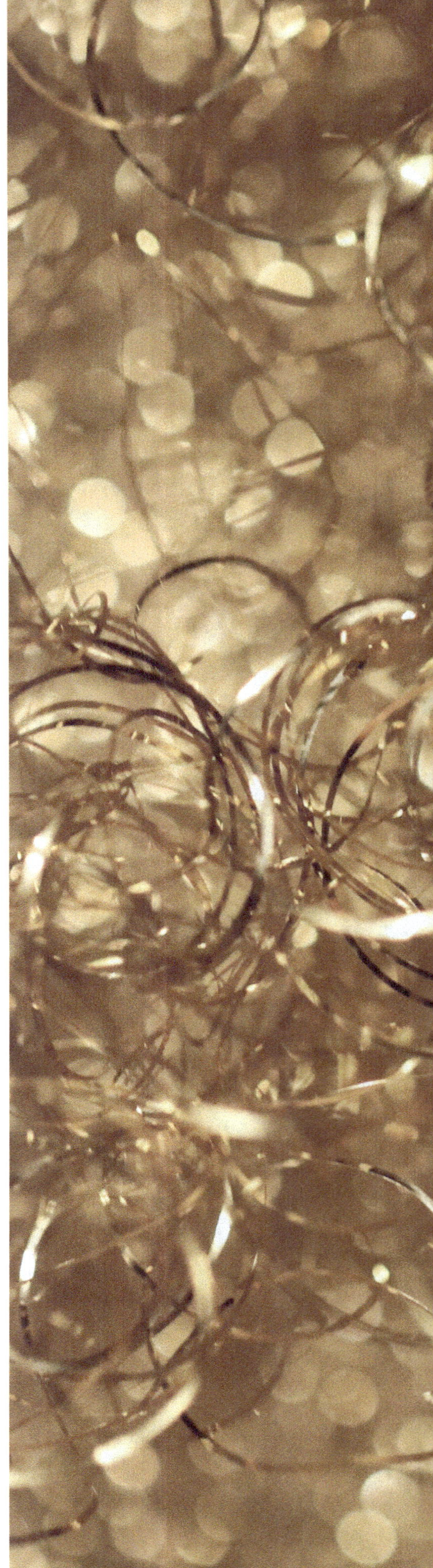

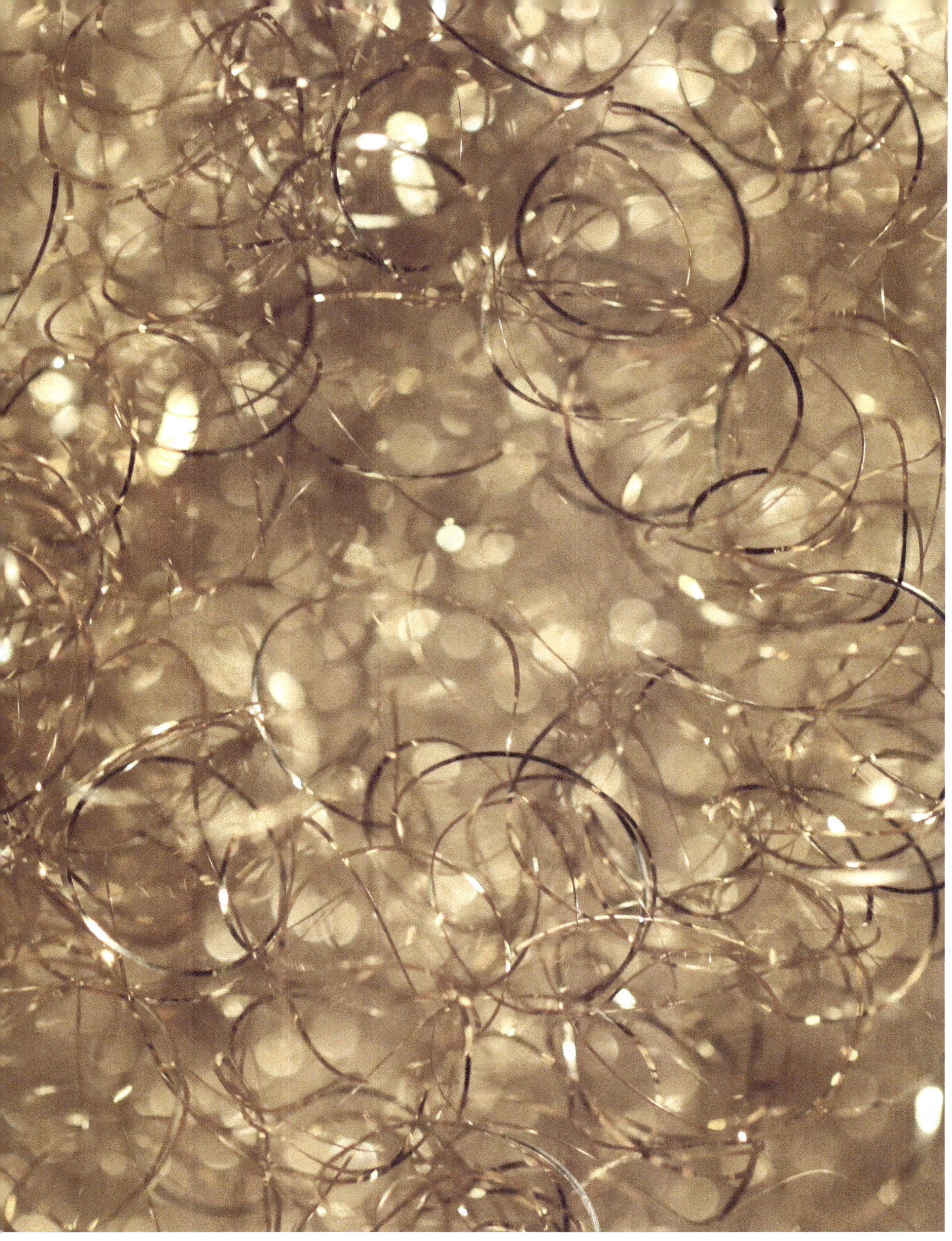

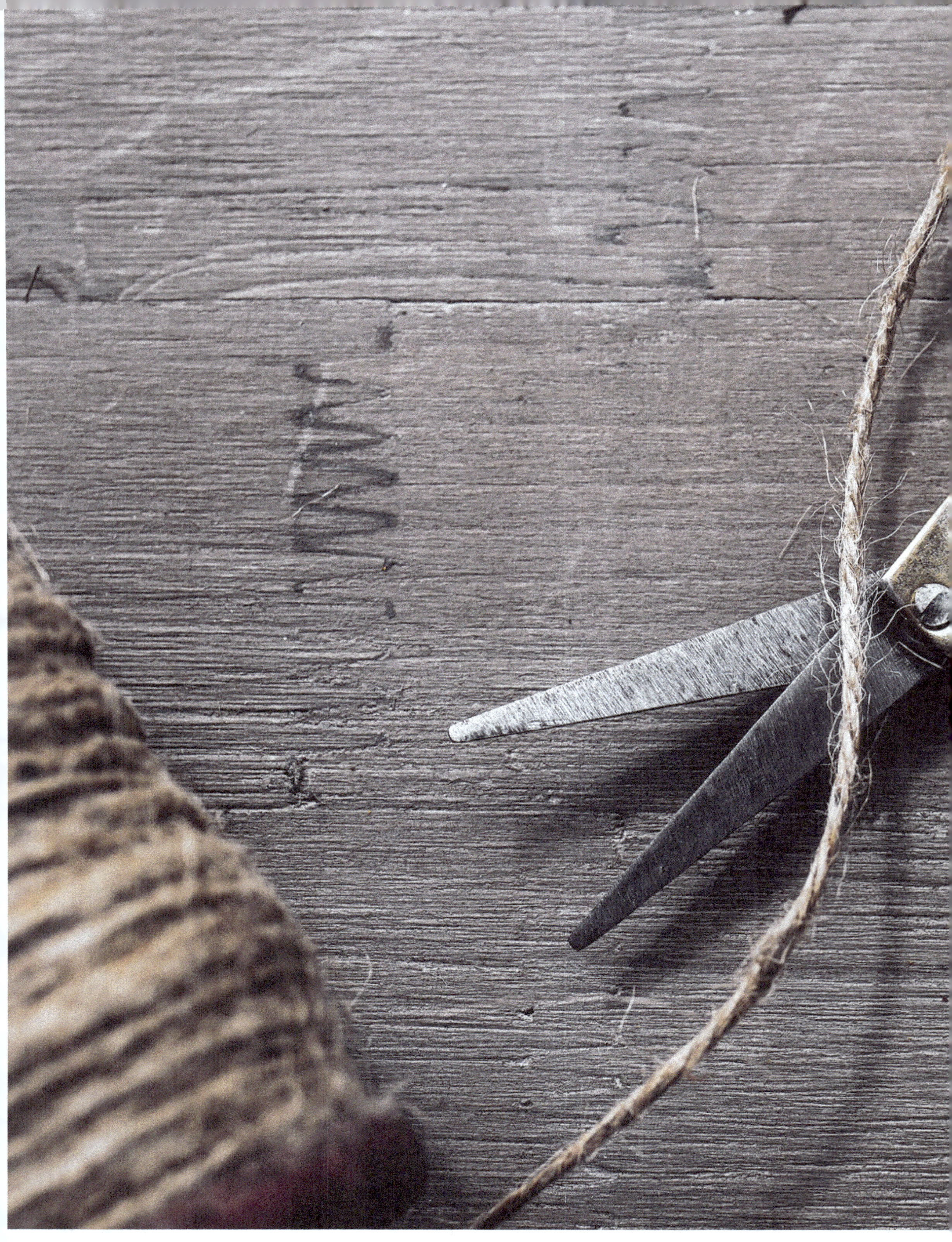

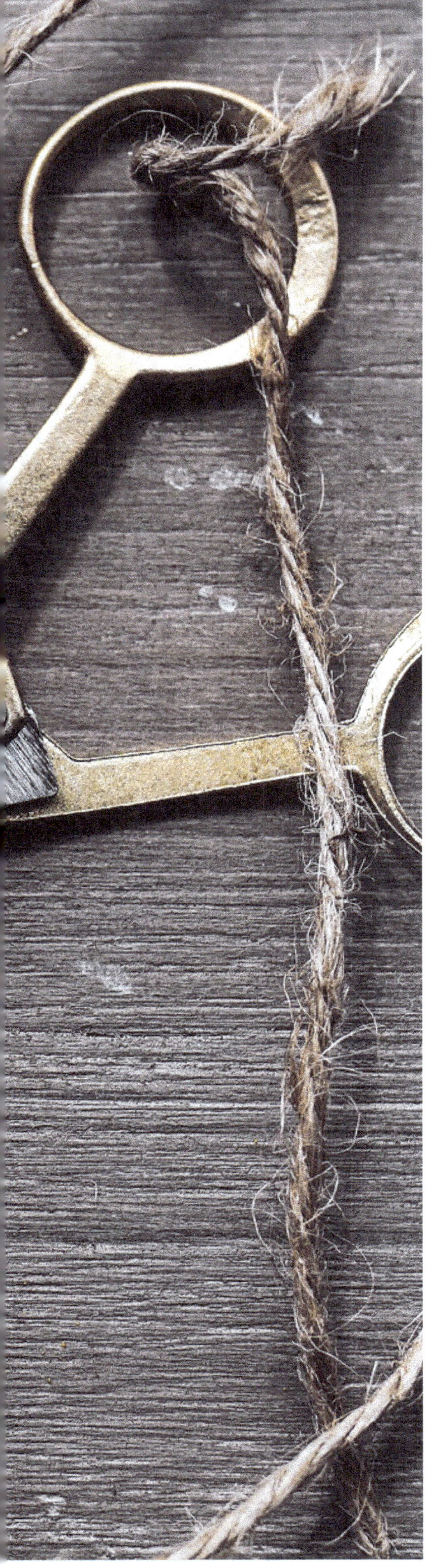

Chapter 2
Common Problems with Cricut machine and how to solve them

<u>Material Tearing or Not Cutting Completely Through</u>

This is the biggest problem with most Cricut users. When this happens, the image is ruined, and you have wasted material. More machines have been returned or boxed up and put away due to this problem rather than any other.

But do not panic; if your paper is not cutting correctly, there are several steps you can take to try and correct the problem.

The most important thing is this: Anytime you work with the blade, TURN YOUR MACHINE OFF.

Make simple adjustments at first. Turn the pressure one number down. Did it help? If not, turn the blade one number down. Also, make sure the mat is free of debris so the edge rides smoothly.

Usually, the thicker the material, the higher the pressure number should be cut through the paper. Do not forget to use the 'Multi-cut' function if you have that option. It may take a little longer to cut 2, 3, or 4 times, but it should cut clean through then.

For those of you using the smaller bugs that do not have that option, here is how to make your multi-cut function. After the image has been cut, do not unload the mat; just hit load paper, repeat last, and cut. You can repeat this sequence 2, 3, or 4 times to ensure your image is completely cut out.

If you are using thinner paper and it is tearing, try reducing the pressure and slowing down the speed. When cutting intricate designs, you have to give the blade enough time to maneuver through the procedure. By slowing it down, it will be able to make cleaner cuts.

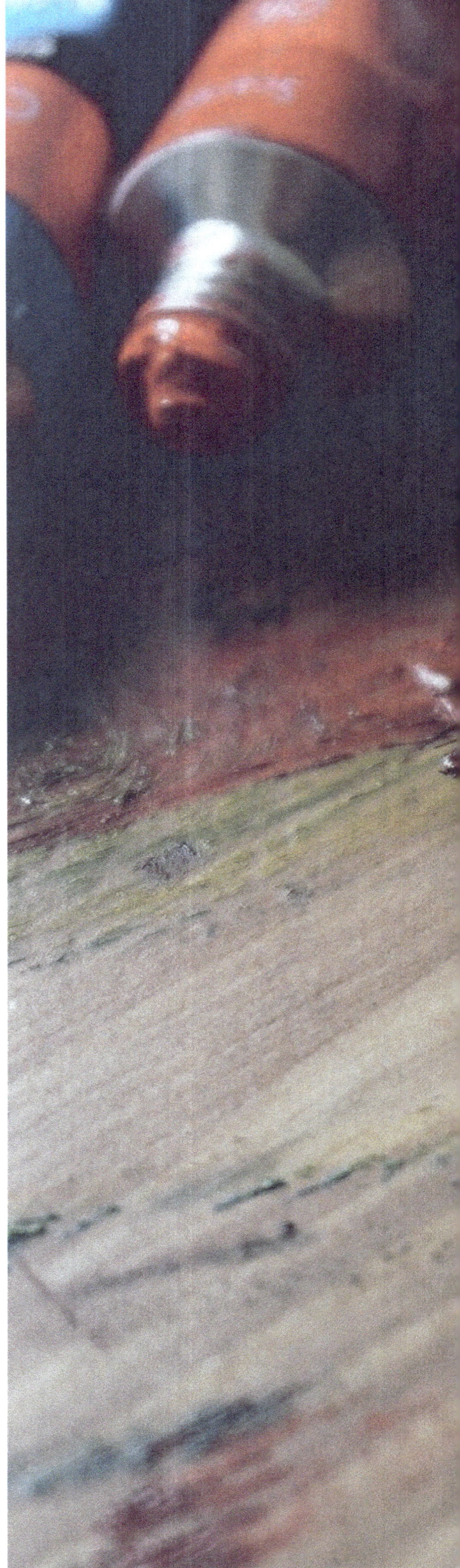

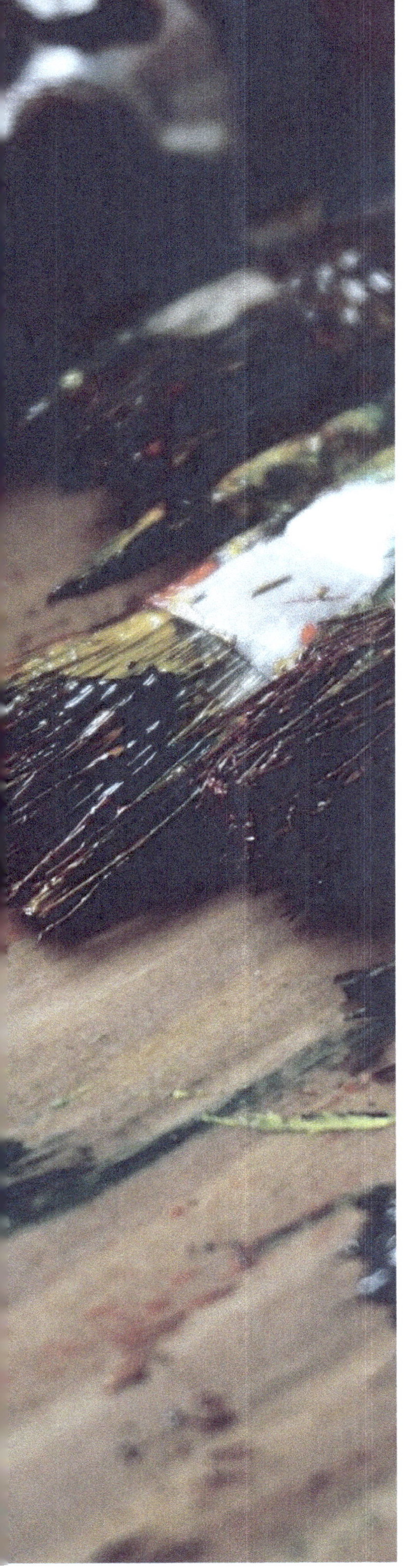

Clean the blade's edge to be sure no fuzz, glue, or scraps of paper are stuck to it.

Make sure the blade is installed correctly. Take it out and put it back, so it is seated firmly. The edge should be steady while it is making cuts. If it makes a shaky movement, it is not installed correctly, or there is a problem with the blade housing.

Be aware that there is a deep-cutting blade for thicker material. You will want to switch to this blade when you are cutting heavy card stock. This will also save wear and tear on your regular knife. Cutting a lot of thick material will wear your blade out quicker than the thinner material and cause you to change it more often.

TRY DIFFERENT MARKERS

Do not feel limited by the Cricut markers. That is right! Using your Cricut machine to write or draw on your project, any marker that will fit will work correctly. Not only are there cheaper options, but the colors and variety of styles are virtually endless. Do not let anyone tell you that you can only use the markers from the Cricut brand. Even though they are of better quality and made for the machine, you are not limited to using them. Just make sure your markers fit.

DOUBLE-CHECK THE SETTINGS

As the testers, this isn't very pleasant, but you have to make sure that your settings are correct and select the right material option. If you are not using the Cricut Design Space, this is easy to forget. When you utilize the software, there is a broad selection of tools to choose from. However, when you are only using a cartridge, the materials are limited. Still, regardless of which set-up you wish to handle the design, you should check your settings twice.

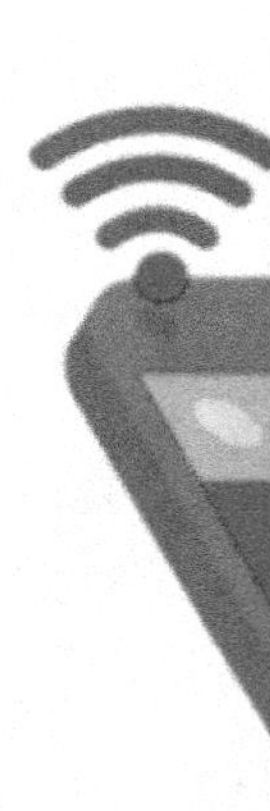

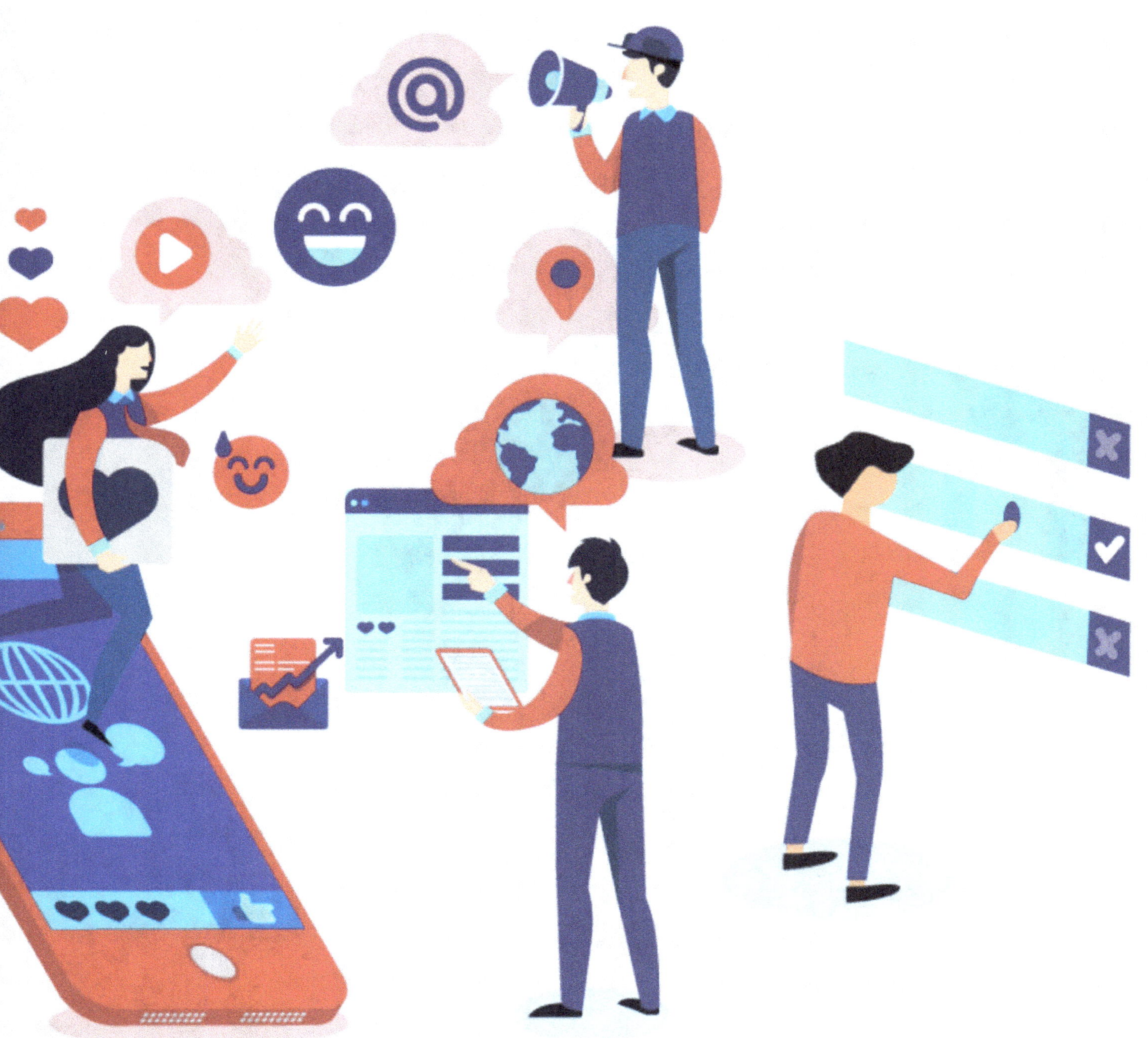

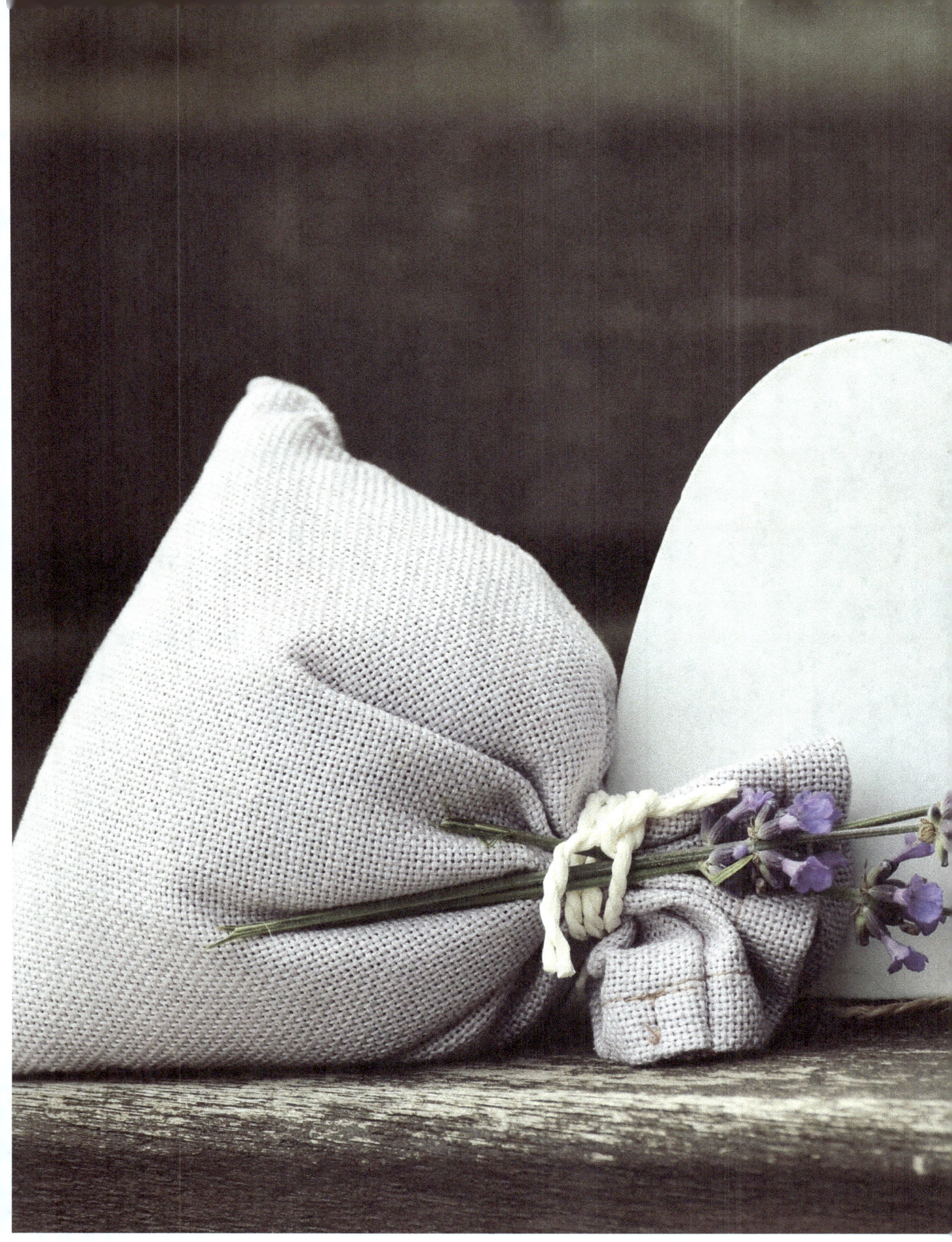

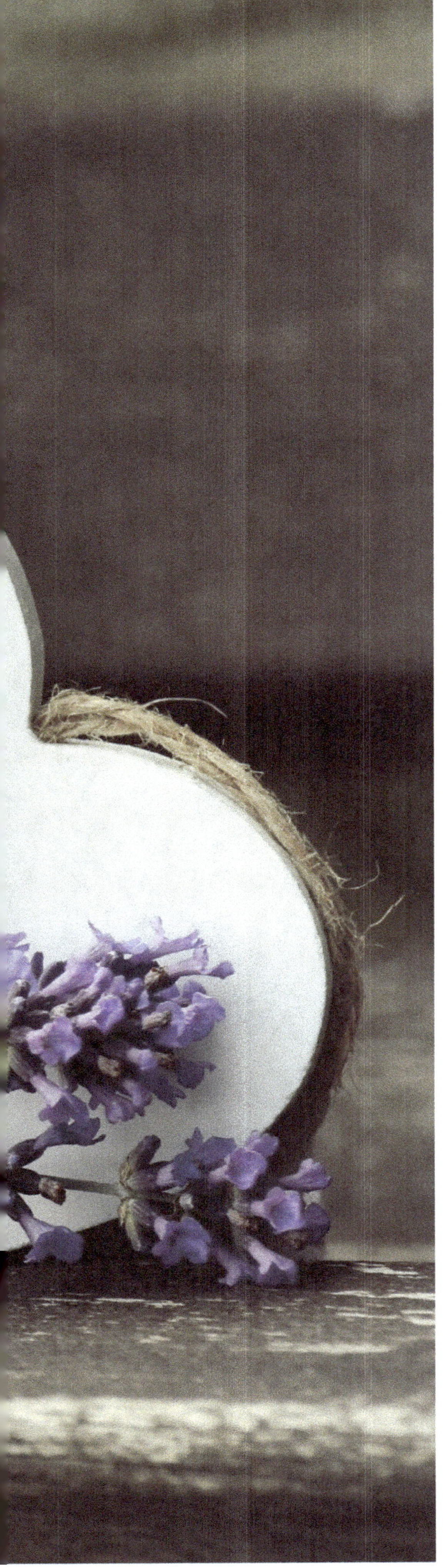

KEEP YOUR BLADES IN A GOOD CONDITION

As you have said before, buy extra blades. Preferably, get one for every material that you are going to cut. In the list of available materials to add to your Cricut purchase, you may see different kinds of blades available for a particular item and that it is sharp at all times. A dull knife is never a good thing, and it will ruin your project as easily as a sharp one will cut it entirely.

EXTEND YOUR MARKERS' SHELF LIFE

Keep your markers upside down with the cap-covered tip facing down when you are not using them. This will ensure that they stay nice and inky for the most extended period. Please do not leave them in your Cricut when you are not using them. Secure the cap and put them away afterward.

PEEL THE MAT AWAY

Avoid your paper curling by peeling the mat away from the paper and not the other way around. Did you wonder why you told you to do this when you were doing your project? This is the reason. Peeling the mat away from the paper will ensure that your paper, or whatever material you are using, from curling. Cricut has a complete cutting guide on their website, which makes cutting your materials more comfortable. Reading that also reduces wastage of materials when you are testing your projects.

You can use 'Glad Press's Seal' as a transfer paper to replace those expensive, original sheets. It is a cheap alternative that works well.

You can use those pen grips that you do not use anymore to adjust a pen and allow it to fit into the pen grip of the Explore family and the Maker machines. Find them if you do not have any lying around the house. You can also utilize the hold of an old pen or even elastic bands to alter the pen's size until it fits snugly in the unit.

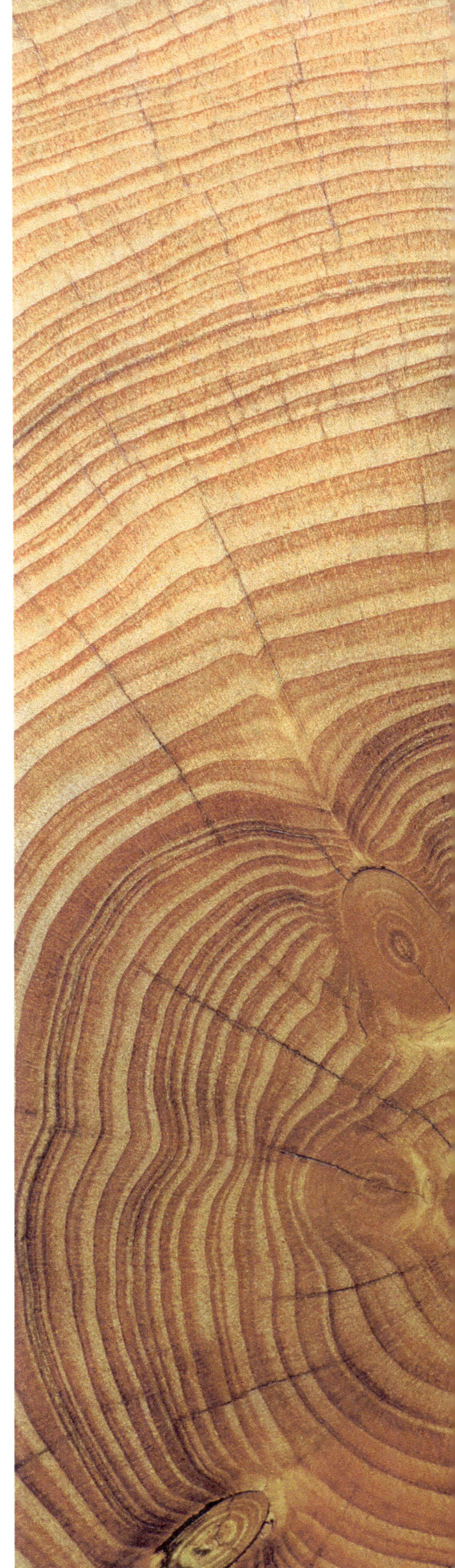

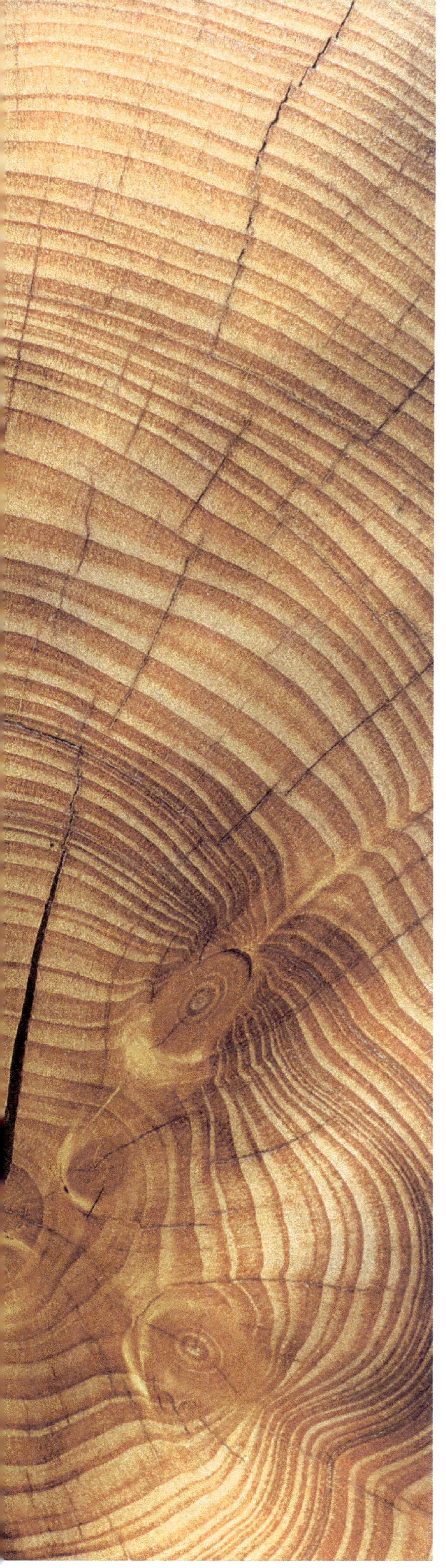

We all know the Cricut mats are not more than a tad expensive. So, what can you do when your mat loses its stickiness? Spraying your carpets with Easy-Tack will instantly restore that feature and make it as good as new (or perhaps even better). Do not forget to cover the non-sticky edges when applying the adhesive to avoid having sticky hands and destroy your project.

If you find that your mat is too tacky in that same breath, you can always gently tap the mat a little, wear the stickiness out a bit, or rub it on your clothes. Just be cautious of pet hair because that will not be easy to get rid of. If you do end up ignoring my warning and making this mistake, the lint roller will do a good job. It might not get all of it out, but it will help significantly.

If your blades are dull and you need to stretch out their shelf life a little, crumble up a piece of aluminum foil until you have a proper ball. Poke the blade into the ball and pull it out again. Repeatedly do this technique for a while so that the edge will have extra few cuts in it. You can repeat this regularly to keep the blades nice. The sharper your knife is, the cleaner your cuts will be. This is a cheap hack with something that you already have at home.

Furthermore, you can use a lint roller to remove those little pieces from your cutouts that might just take you all day to remove by hand. It might not snag all of those pesky bits, but the tool will reduce the number of fragments that you will have to pluck out manually. This is also helpful for removing excess glitters from your project so that they do not fly around the entire house and give you headaches for years to come (yes, we all know terrible glitter is). As mentioned earlier, it is also great for removing hairs from projects, as well as mats. There are communities on social media that are great for novice and advanced Cricutters. You can ask any questions, and the members of the

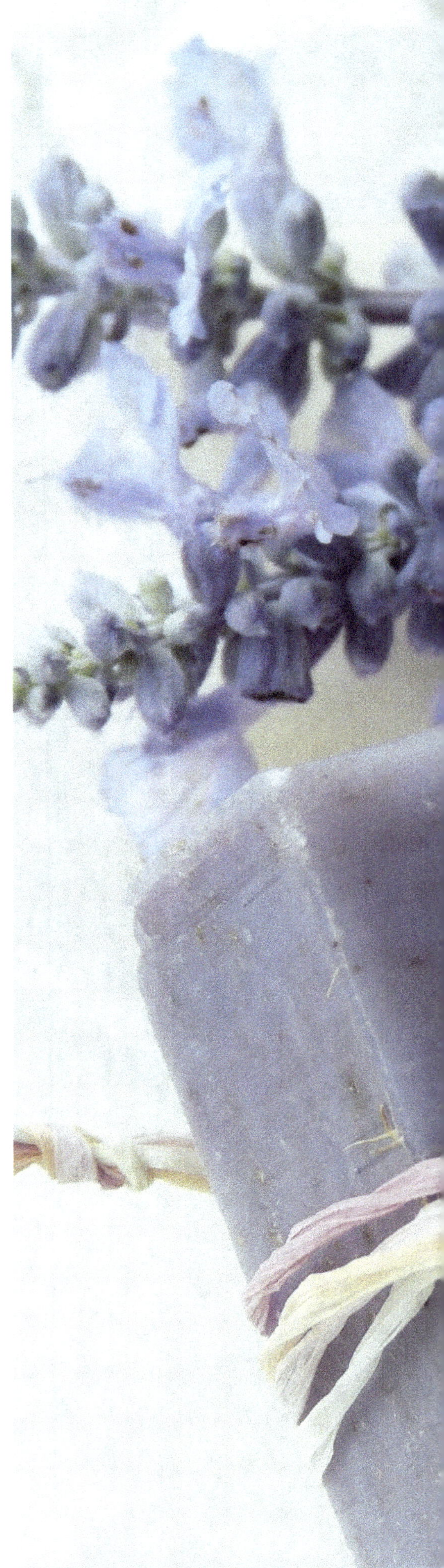

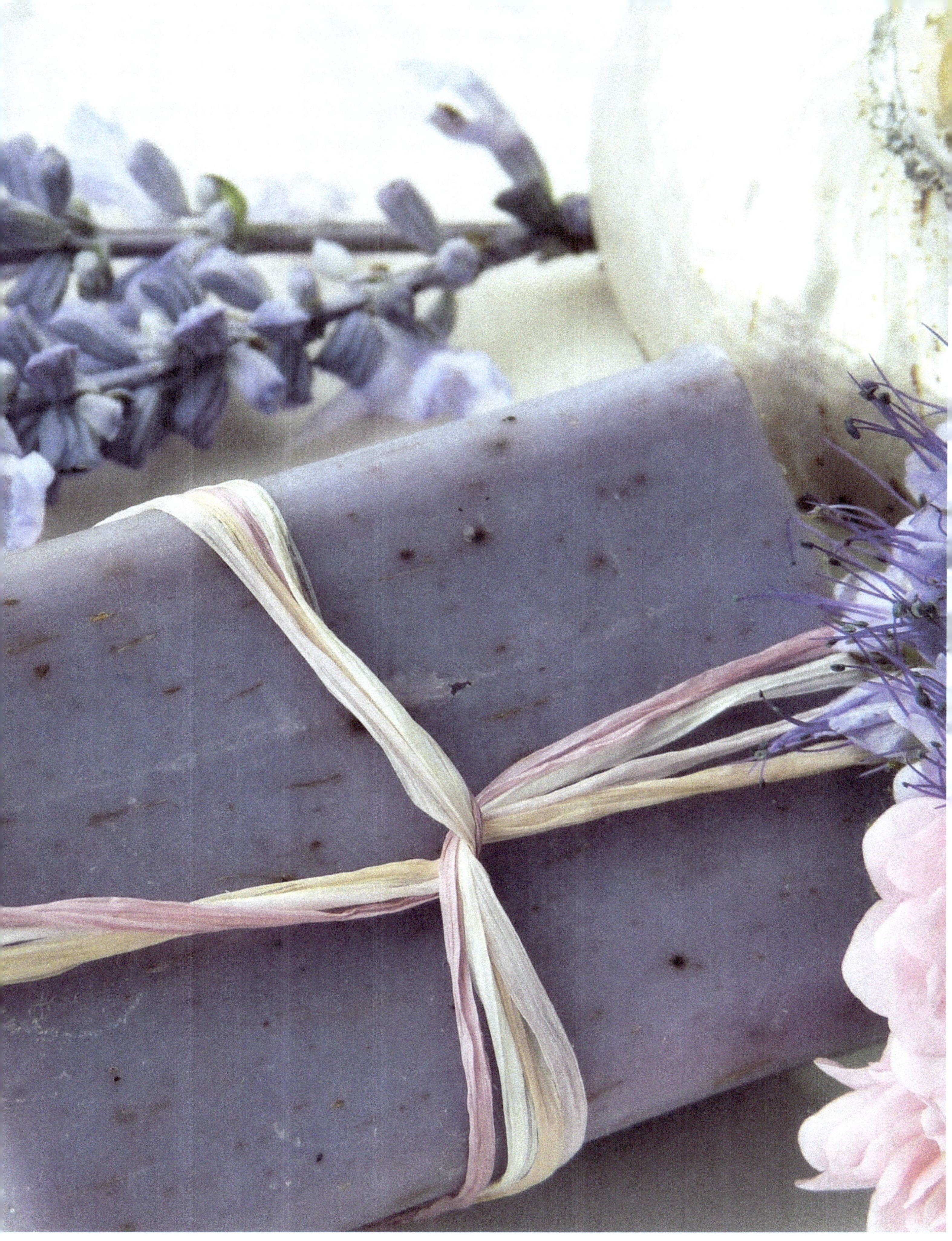

community will do everything they can to help you as they have been be-ginners too. Everyone is super lovely in these groups, and you will not make a mistake if you decide to join any of them.

Read the manual too. Oh, it is a te-dious thing. However, it is essential to learn your machine in and out before you start pressing random buttons. It was a real problem for me to figure out what to do at the time, so make the effort of reading your manual. It will help you.

Machine Freezing

Remember always to turn your ma-chine off when you switch cartridges. When you change cartridges, leaving the device on is called 'hot swapping' and can sometimes cause the engi-ne to freeze. This is more of an issue with the older models and does not seem to apply to Expression 2.

You know how quirky electronic ga-dgets can be, so give your machine

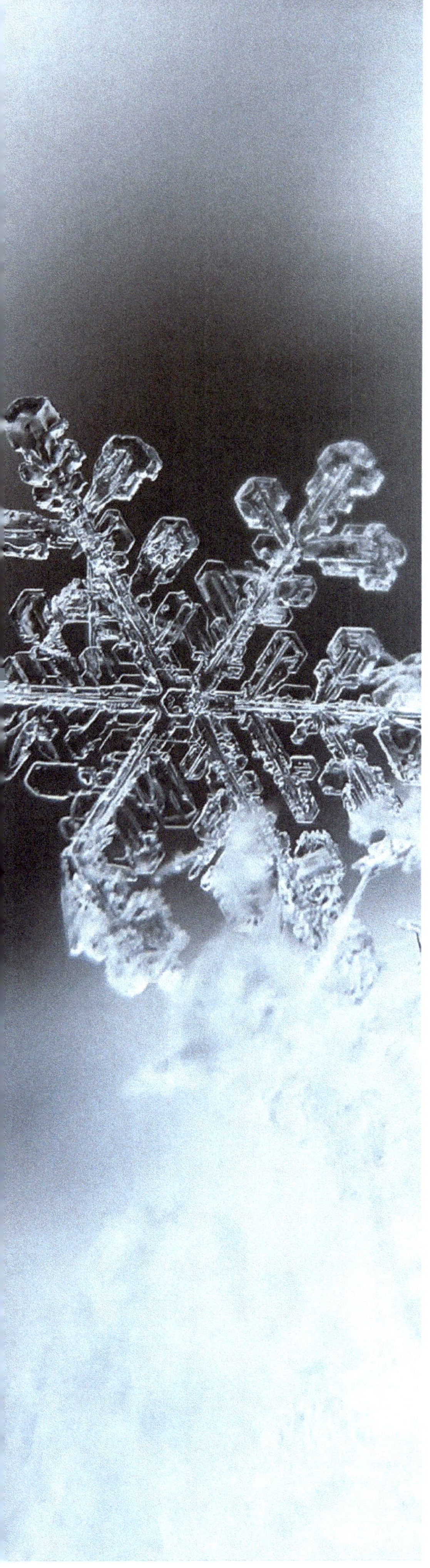

rest for five or ten minutes every hour. If you work for several hours continuously, your machine might overheat and freeze up.

Turn the machine off and take a break. Restart it when you come back, and it should be fine. Then remember not to rush programming the device and give it an occasional rest.

Do not press a long list of commands quickly. If you give it too much information too fast, it will get confused in the same way a computer sometimes does and will simply freeze up. Instead of typing in one long phrase, try dividing up your words into several cuts.

If you are using special feature keys, make sure you press them first before selecting the letters.

Power Problems

If you turn your machine on and nothing happens, the power adapter may be at fault. Jiggle the power

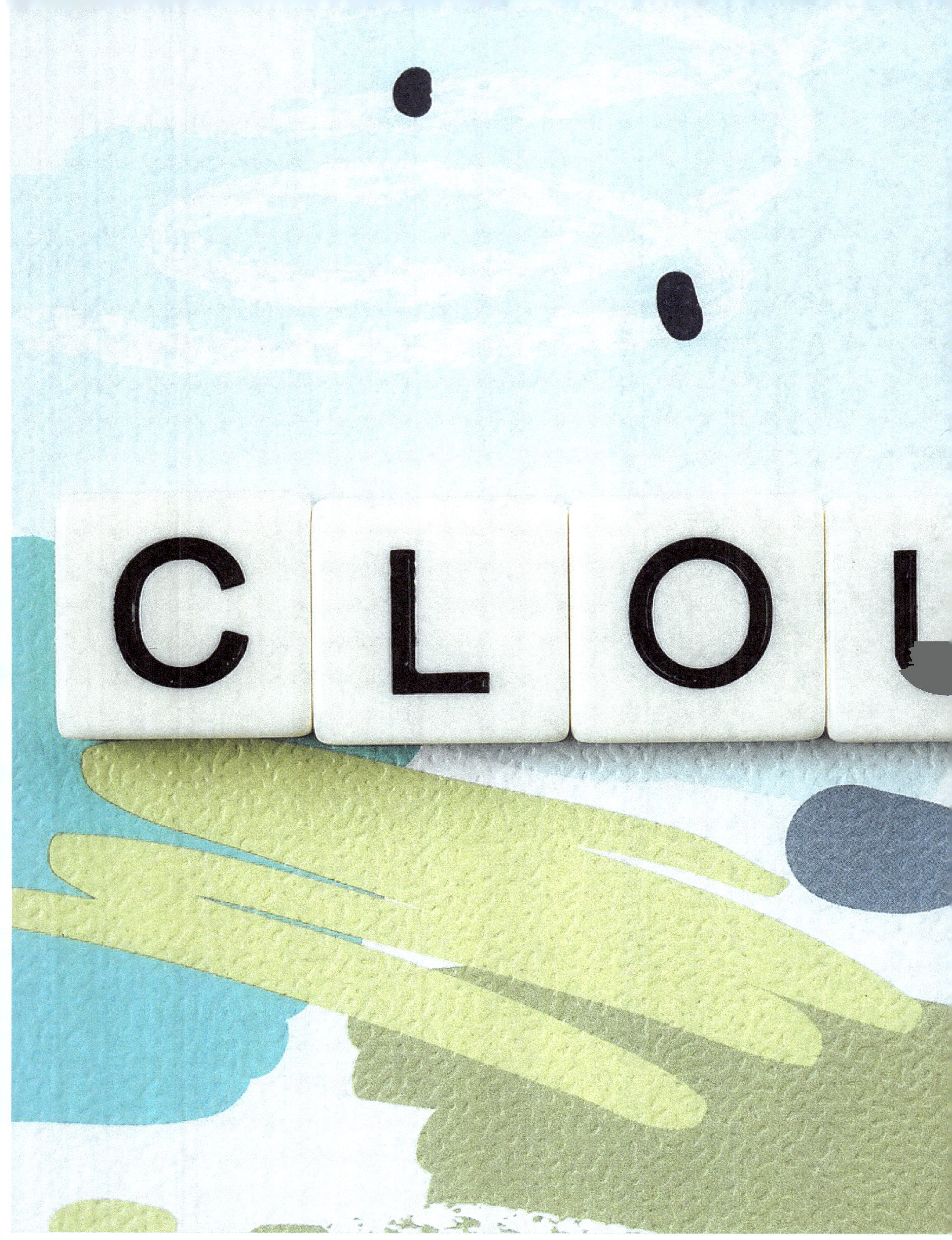

C L O U

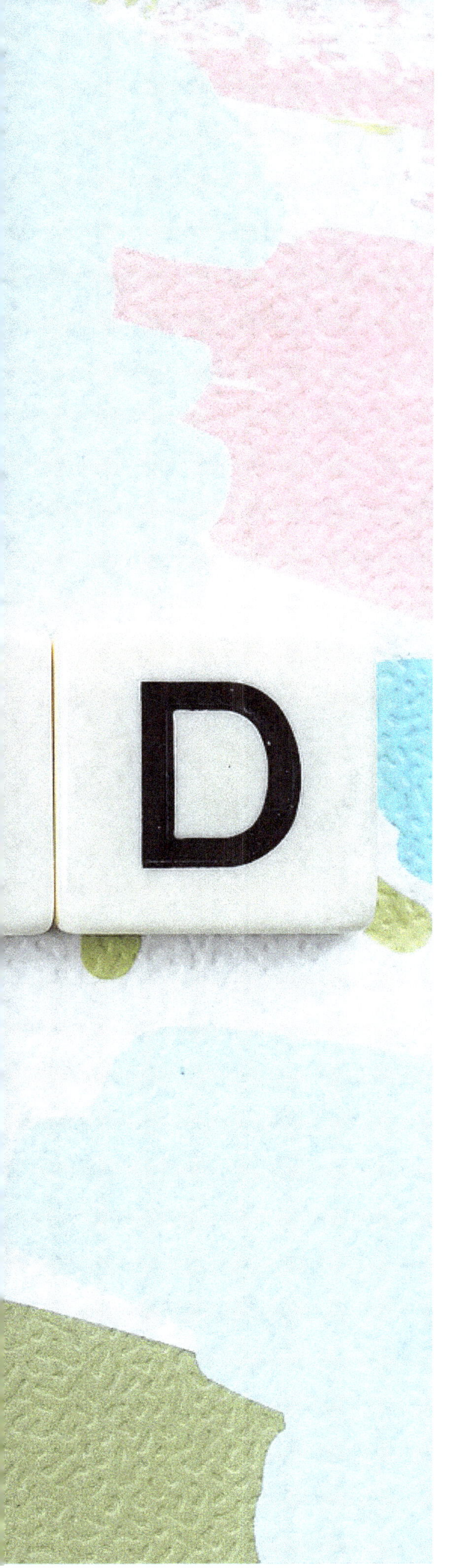

cord at the outlet and connect to the device to make sure it is firmly connected. Ideally, you want to test the adapter before buying a new one. Swap cards with a friend and see if that fixed the problem. Replacement adapters can be found on eBay by searching for Cricut adapter power supply.

The connection points inside the machine may also pose a problem; here is how to test that. Hold down the plug where it inserts into the back of the machine and turn it on. If it powers up, then the problem is inside the device, and the connection points will have to be soldered again.

If the machine powers up but will not cut, then try a hard reset. See the resource section for step-by-step instructions on resetting your machine. Here are a few tips, especially for Expression 2 users. Have you turned on your machine, you watch it light up and hear it gearing up, but when you try to cut, nothing happens? Or are you stuck on the welcome screen, or the LCD screen is unresponsive?

Well, here are two quick fixes to try. First, try a hard reset, sometimes called the 'Rainbow Screen Reset' to recalibrate your die cutter. If that does not resolve the problem, you are going to have to restore the settings.

To help cut down on errors, try to keep your machine updated. When an update is available, you should receive a message encouraging you to install the latest version.

For those of you using third-party software that is no longer compatible with the Cricut, you probably already know that updating your machine may disable that software.

When you cut heavy paper and your Expression 2 shuts down, try switching to the regular paper setting, and use the multi-cut function.

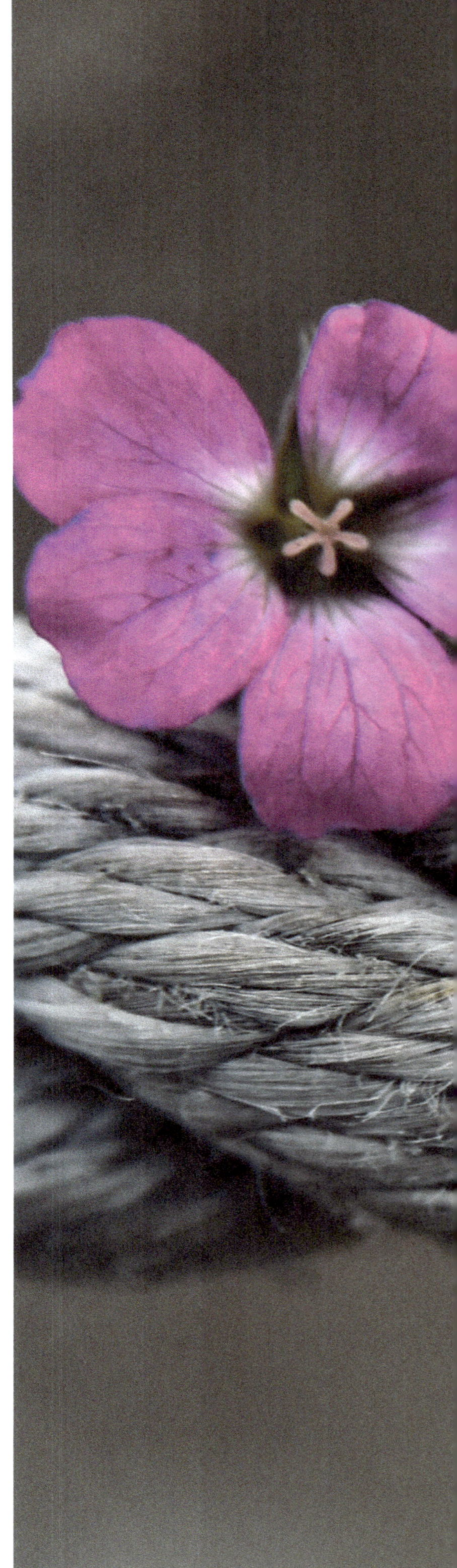

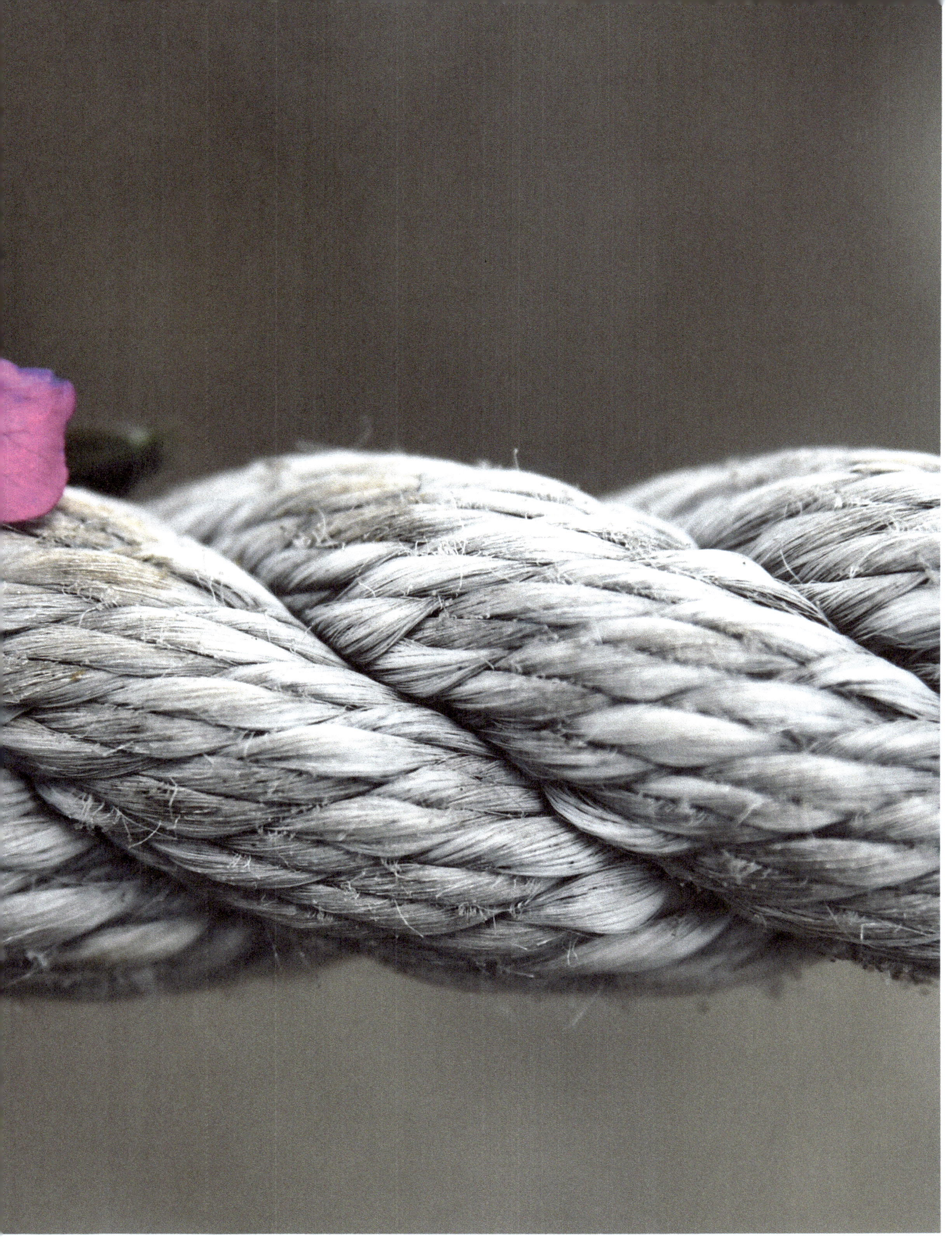

Carriage Will Not Move

If the carriage assembly does not move, check whether the belt is broken or the car fell off the track. Provo Craft does not sell replacement parts, which is nuts, so try to find a compatible belt at a vacuum repair shop.

If the wheels have fallen off the track, remove the plastic cover, look for a tiny screw by the wheel, and unscrew it. You now should be able to move the wheel back on track.

Unresponsive Keyboard

If you are sure you are pressing the keys firmly, you have a cartridge inserted correctly and a mat loaded ready to go, but the keypad is still not accepting your selection; the problem may be internal.

You will have to remove the keyboard and check if the display cable is connected to the keypad and the

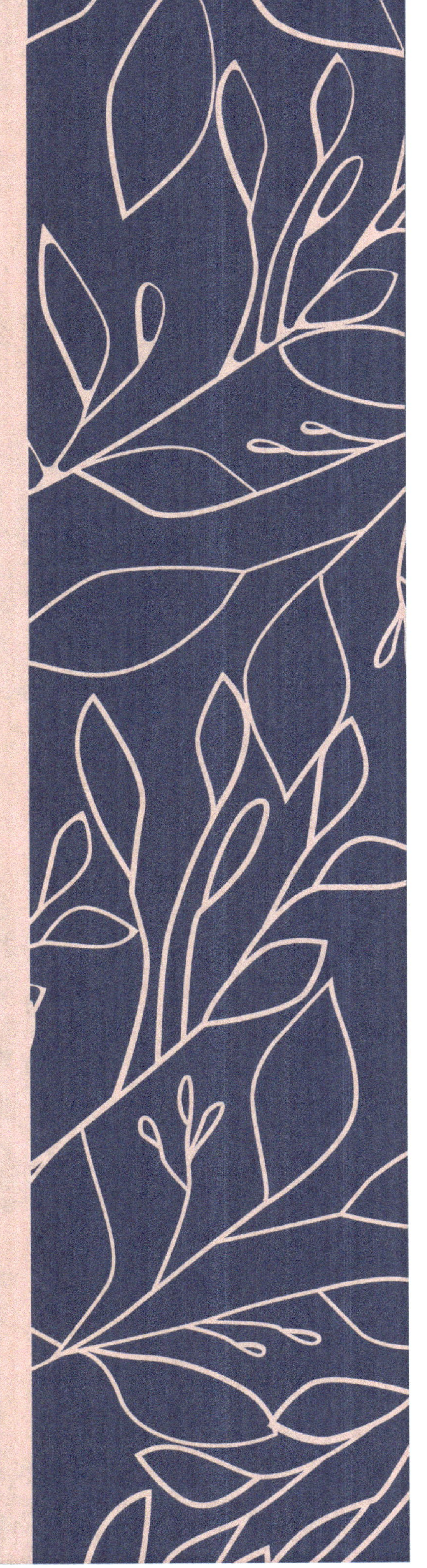

motherboard. If the connections are secure, you have a circuit board problem, and repairs are beyond this book's scope.

An important reminder, please do not attempt any repairs unless your machine is out of warranty.

Weird LCD Screen

The LCD screen is now showing strange symbols or blank; after doing a firmware update, try rerunning the update and make sure your selections are correct.

When the image you choose is more significant than the mat or paper size you selected, the preview screen will look grayed out instead of showing the picture. So, increase the paper and mat size, or decrease the size of your image.

Also, watch out for the gray box effect when using the center point feature. Move the start position down until you see the image appear. The same

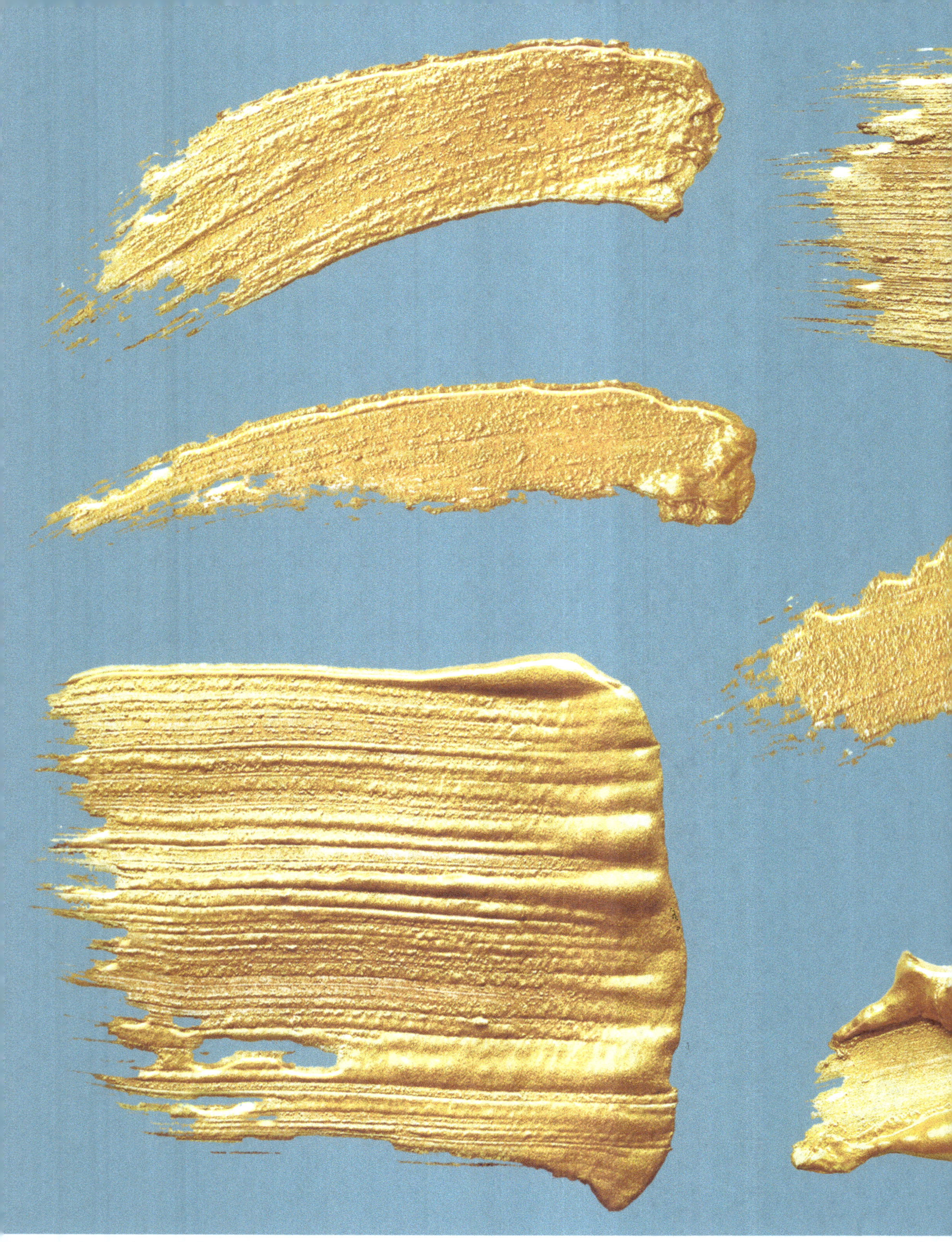

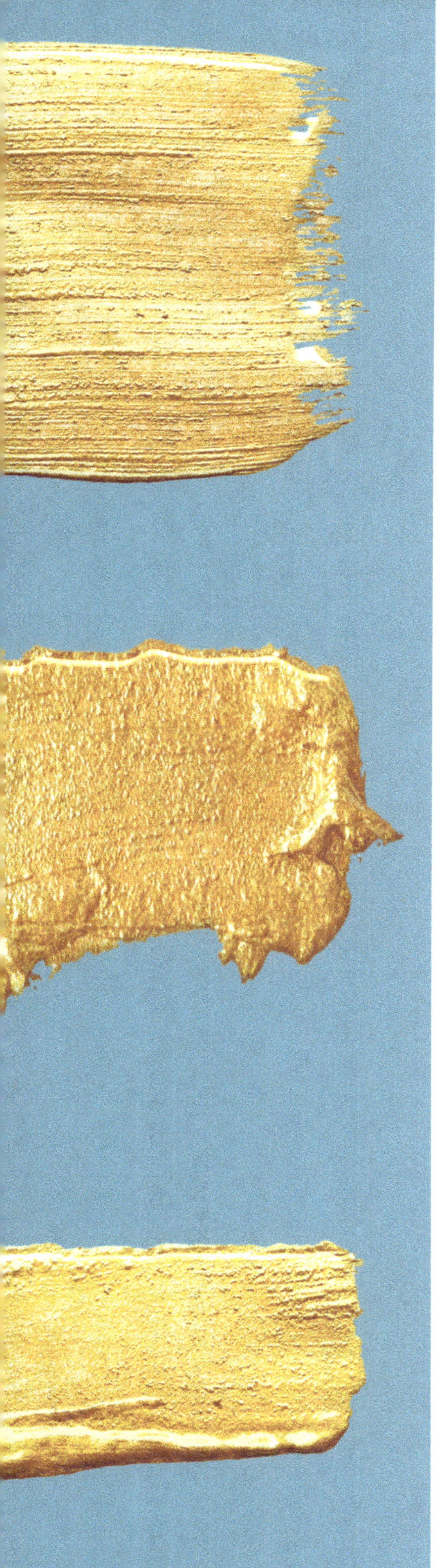

thing may happen when using the 'Fit to Length' part. Try changing to landscape mode and shorten the length size until the image appears. Occasionally using the undo button will cause the preview screen to turn black; unfortunately, the only thing to do is turn the machine off. Your work will be lost, and you have to start again.

Cartridge Errors

Sometimes dust or debris accumulates in the cartridge port; gently blow out any paper fiber that may have collected in the opening. Make sure the contact points are clean and that nothing is preventing the cartridge from being read correctly.

With any electrical machine, overheating can be a problem. If you get a cartridge error after using your device for a while, turn it off, and let it cool down for about fifteen minutes.

If you thought you could use your

cartridges with your Expression 2, think again. You will get an error message because you can only use the art cartridges you can cut with; the colors and patterns cartridges are for printing. Even brand-new items, fresh out of the box, can be defective. If you see a cartridge error 1, 2, 3, 4, 5, 6, 9, or 99, call customer service and tell them the name, serial number, and error message number, and they may replace the cartridge.

Internet Connection

The primary reason Cricut making machine has issues is a poor internet connection. Cricut Design Space software or app requires fast, stable upload and download speeds to comfortably send and receive information when a project is going on.

Should the connection become inconsistent or below what it needed, the software may start hanging or freezing? The developers say Space needs

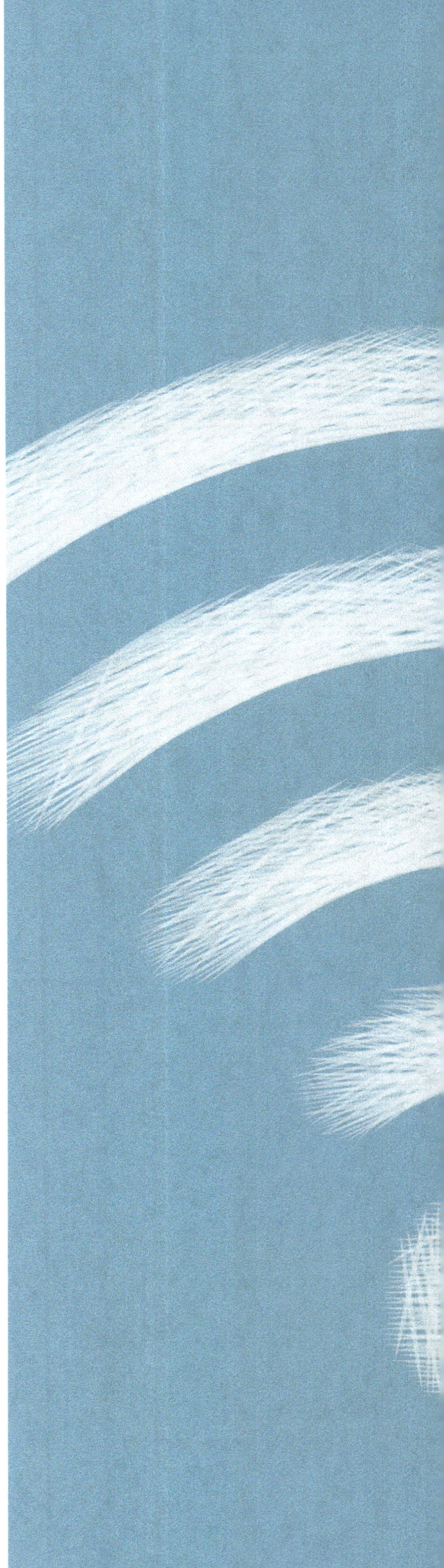

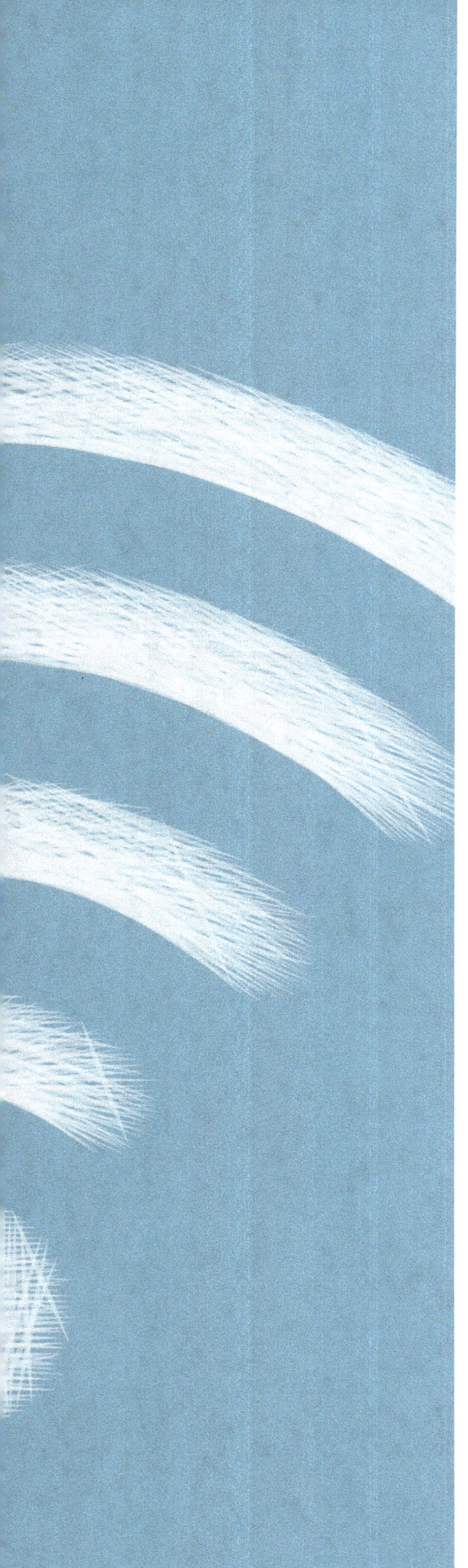

a download speed of no less than 2 Mbps and an upload speed of 3 Mbps to function correctly.

If your internet connection does not work this fine, consult with your service provider to help you with a new router, modem, or subscription plan. However, do check the specifications on your computer to see if it matches the required speed. You may find that the problems are from your Mac. To run Design Space, you need to have Mac OS X10.12 or higher, with 83 GHz CPU, 4 GB RAM< 50 MB available hard disk space, and Bluetooth connection. For Windows computers, it needs to be version 8 or higher, have Intel Core or AMD processors, 4 GB RAM, 500 MB free hard disk space, and Bluetooth connection. If these are in place, you've hit the ground running already.

Don't Do Cut Tests

Unless you produce the material your-

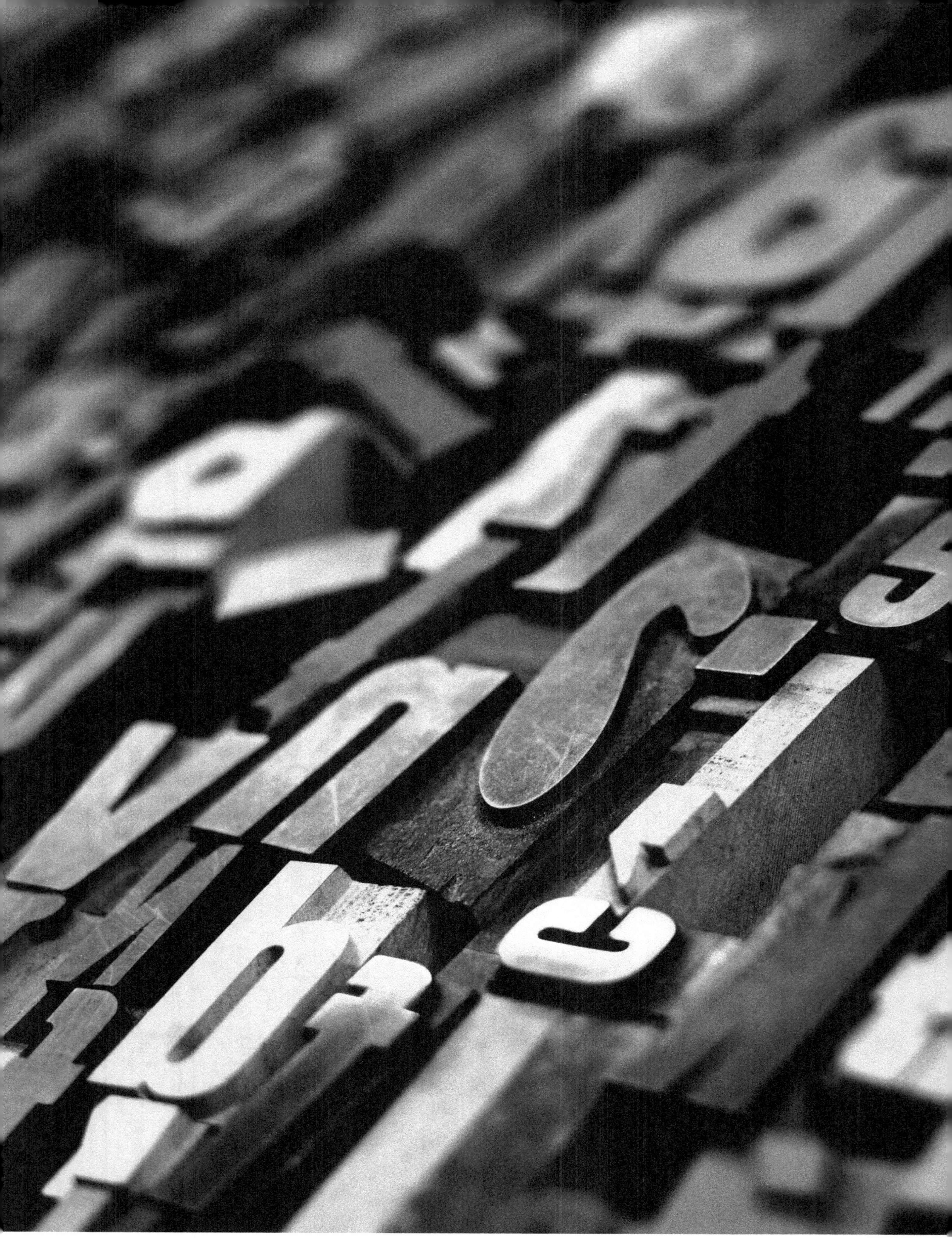

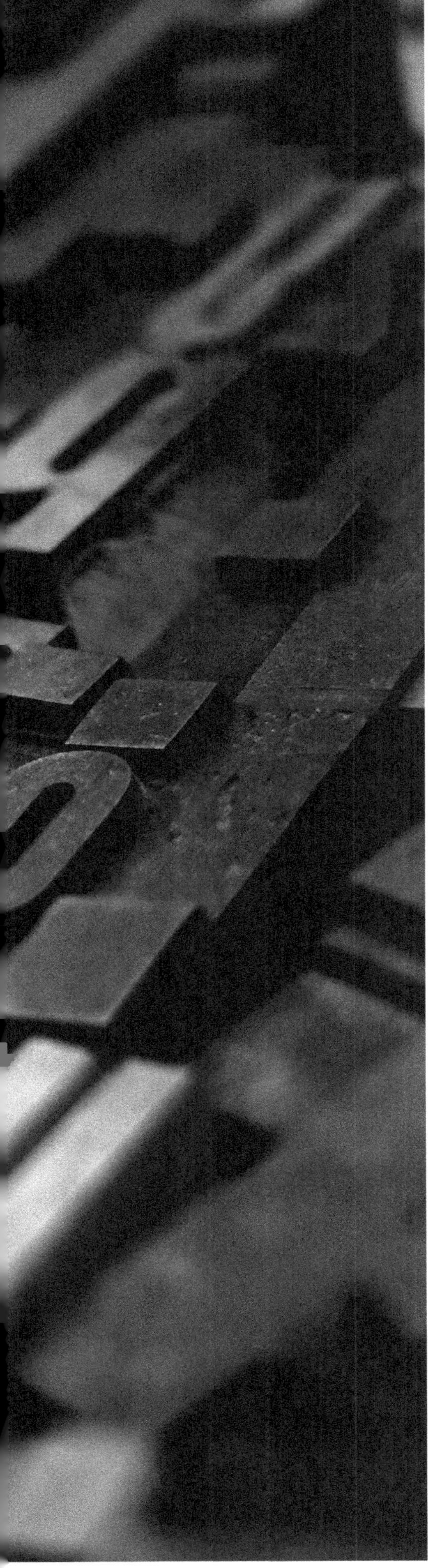

self and have a lot to spend, doing cut tests should be a no-no. The best thing to do is perform one or more small test sections each time you insert the blade holder to cut new material. Rather than assuming that the recommended settings for a specific material are always correct, suppose they are not, just to be safe.

Many things factor into how the material is cut, from the sharpness of the blade to the condition of the carpet, the effect of moisture, and the dye color used in the material.

Are you unable to do a proper test? Well, there is a chance the rest of your project will be a waste of time. Another good idea would be to choose a similar form, like the one used on your project.

In other words:

When you cut a title, use a small letter as the cut shape.

When cutting a rhinestone pattern, test a small pattern with ten circles of similar size to those used in the rhinestone design.

When you cut large, simple shapes,
you can use a basic form such as a
circle, a square, or a heart.

Stabilization in Cutting

When you have your material placed
in a way the blade cannot penetrate
it, the material will not move through
the sharpness. The cut parts will not
fall out of the material, even while
the cutting continues.

Like many heat sealable products, vinyl
has a backing layer that serves as a
stabilizer. But for paper products, stabili-
zation is a must. Press on a clean and
sticky carpet that cannot be penetrated
by the blade but can only be scra-
tched by the tip.

Supposing you do not have any cle-
an-cut, it may be best to observe the
cutting mat closely, so confirm whether
there is a lack. This usually occurs at
the point where pinch rollers run over
the carpet.

Nonetheless, it could be a mere loss

of adhesiveness due to accumulation and the interference of invisible material fibers. You can wash the cutting mats with some warm water and soap. This way, the fibers can be absorbed and washed away.

The glue on the carpet will not be removed still. After drying, the surface would become quite sticky again. Anyway, check the entire mat surface and throw some more non-repositionable adhesive to the areas that do not stick.

You can use a Goo Gone or Duck Adhesive Remover to do a total removal, after which you will apply a new film.

Blade Problems

Increasing blade exposure does not solve incision issues. Contrary to conventional opinion, a larger blade does not deliver a better cut.

The quality of the blade should be commensurate with the thickness of the material. If any of your blades are

exposed, you will cut the carpet un-
necessarily and have more crumples,
teardrops, and incomplete incisions.
Should the blade's end protrude into
the carpet, the material will likely get
separated from the carpet, destabilized,
and eventually ruptured. So, do not
leave too much blade on the blade
holder. Leave only as necessary.
Another costly problem is the assump-
tion the blade is chipped already. On
high-force machines, a knife can hit
a bigger edge. It does not only pierce
the materials but gets pushed into the
carpet to hot the hard surface.
This means that chips are not very
common. They should not be consi-
dered if you somehow end up with
incomplete cuts. On the one hand, a
more significant number of the shred-
ded blade cut no material at all.
To determine if the blade has flaked
off, scan to magnify the image, ulti-
mately facilitating the inspection of the
blade's tip. Some knives come with a
low reduction system to reduce offset

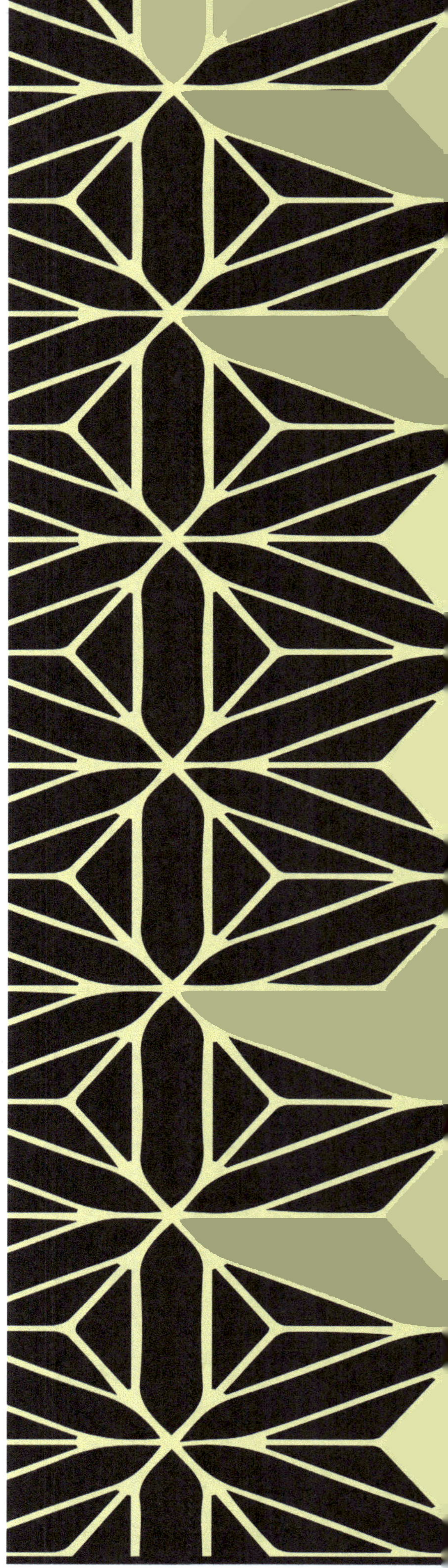

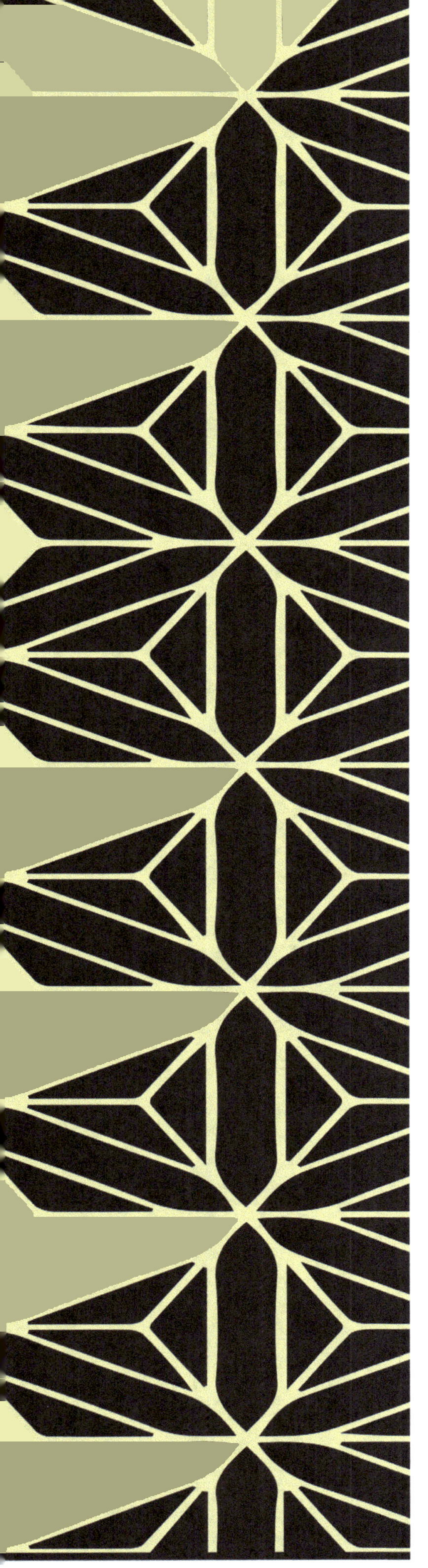

size and create room for smaller details. Do not mistake a broken sword with the reduction incidence.

If you don't understand what the blade offset does and doesn't do, there is a chance you will blame the misalignment for the cutting problems.

Most of the time, the rounded, bubbled corners or hanging panes are entirely forgotten. These cuts are hardly have anything to do with the debris on which the blade starts and stops. So, you need to be careful enough to understand what this parameter is responsible for.

For knives with restricted ranges, the settings are built into the firmware. Regardless, if you see this parameter in your Design Space, you must try to understand it. Blade offset occurs when the blade's tip is at a slightly disparaging location with the center of the blade shaft.

Chapter 3
Tips and Tricks

Get More Accessories

Some tools can help you repair your mat for sale on the Cricut website, but if you are just starting and you are still learning about materials and pressures, chances are you're going to ruin a mat or two. The same goes for the blades. If you practice as much as you should with your machine to get the hang of it, you have to buy extra blades. Rips in your projects become more frequent when you have a blunt blade. This is something that you want to avoid. So, when purchasing your very first Cricut, make sure to add the said items to your cart as well. There's nothing as wrong as running out of materials while you're in the middle of a project.

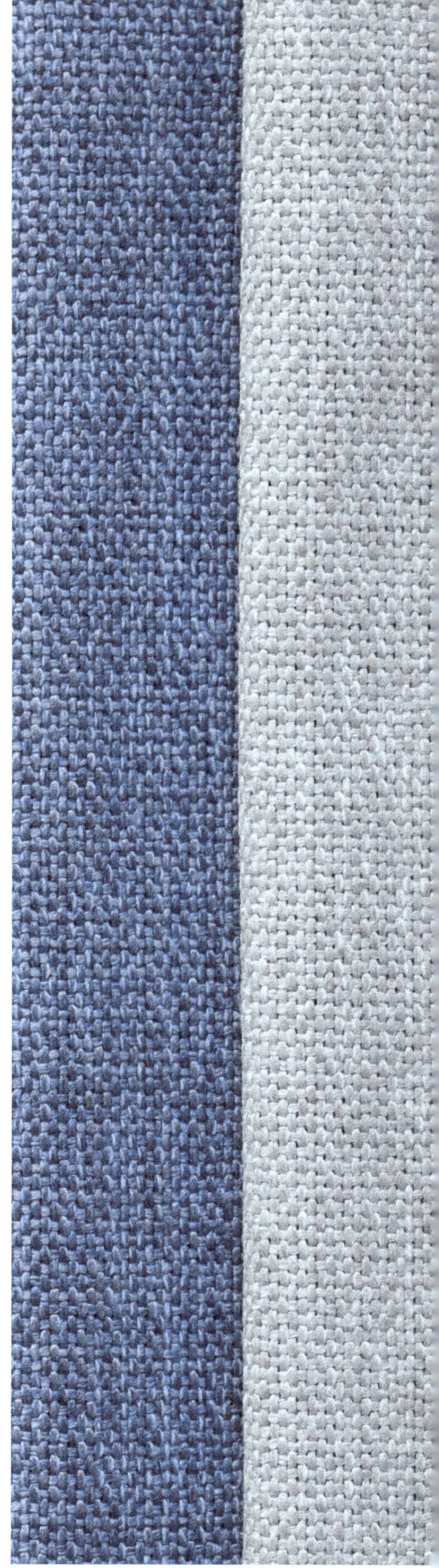

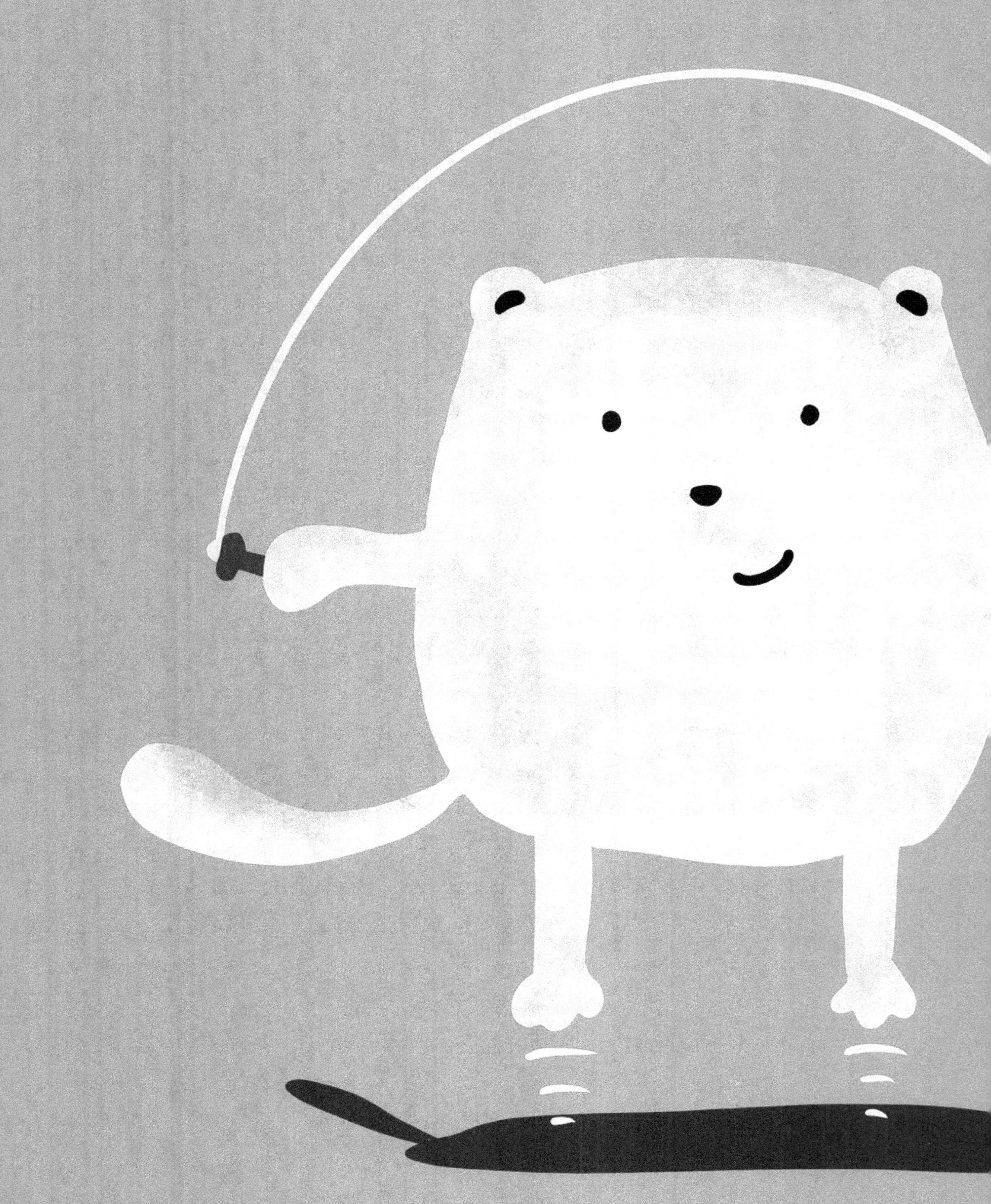

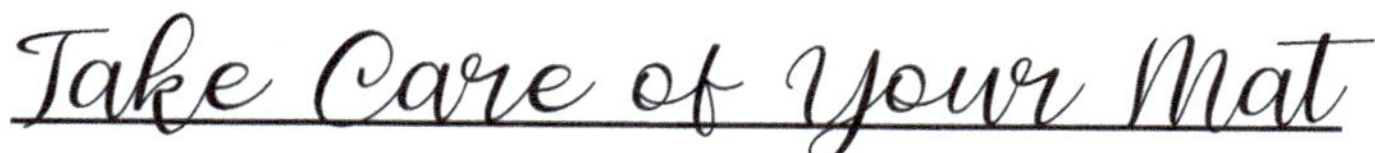

Take Care of Your Mat

If you don't already own one, well, now you know. The point is that the alcohol gets rid of the stickiness and leaves you with just a direct old mat. If the material doesn't stick to it, the paper, vinyl, and others will all move around while the blade is trying to cut through, and it will end in a disaster.

So, your best bet will be to use non-alcoholic wipes. Baby wipes are perfect for this. Just scrub down your mat with it when you feel like it is getting a bit iffy, and you're good to go. You wipe the mat after every use to be sure that there will be nothing stuck to it the next time you want to use the machine

Don't Be Lazy

Test those projects first! Testing is key to mastering the Cricut even when you feel like you've already gotten the hang of it. It never hurts to assess your projects before doing the final cut or print. It might seem tedious, and I'll be the first to admit that I'm sluggish where things that consume my time are concerned, but this is a useful tip. Test before you cut. Make it a habit of yours. It should come without a thought. It might just save

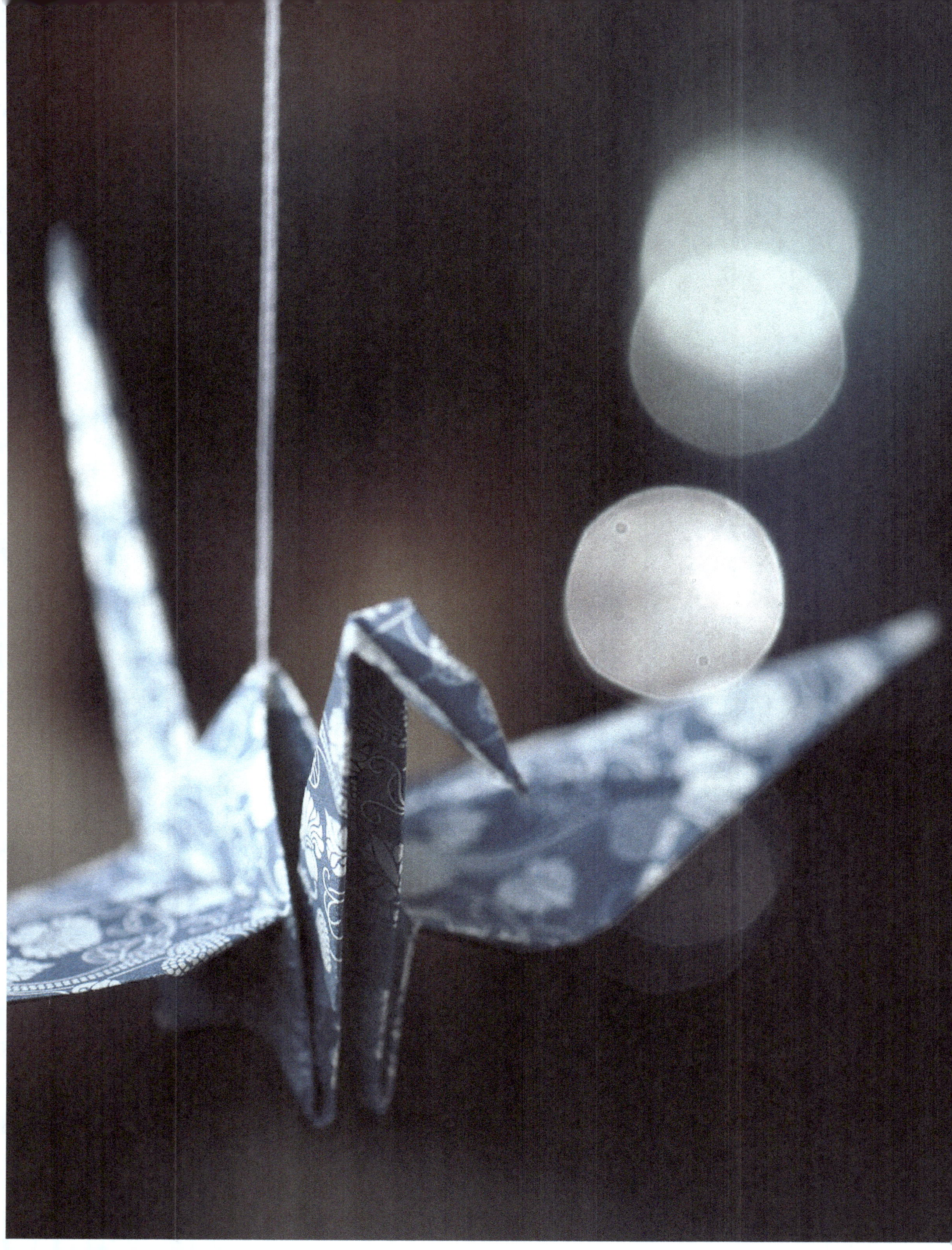

you a lot of time and material too. Instead of doing the whole project at once, do a small element of it first. If it doesn't work, you won't need to wait for it to finish before fixing the settings and cutting the new design. It will also save you the pain of losing the material you wanted to use for the project itself.

Think of Fabrics

Fabrics are challenging to work with. Let's get it out there in the open you have given up on cutting materials completely. It's not that you don't think it can be done - I've seen people make fantastic fabric items with the Cricut - but you don't have the patience to sew, so it is pretty much useless for me to try figuring it out. A friend of mine owns the Cricut Maker as well, though, and let me tell you; she is a beast when it comes to cutting the patterns and sewing them afterward! She made me cut multiple items that you just basically stuck together with a glue gun, and it worked perfectly. It was much more efficient than doing it by hand. If you are looking to cut fabric, the Cricut Maker is your best bet. The Explore family is right for it, but the range of material it can cut is limited compared to the Cricut Maker. Don't even look at the other

machines. You're welcome for that little piece of advice.

Try Different Markers

Don't feel limited by the Cricut markers. That's right! When you are using your Cricut machine to write or draw on your project, any marker that will fit will work correct- ly. Not only are there cheaper options, but the colors and variety of styles are virtually endless. Don't let anyone tell you that you can only use the markers from the Cricut brand. Even though they are of better quality and made for the machine, you are not limited to using them. Just make sure your markers fit.

Double-Check the Settings

As the testers, this isn't very pleasant, but you have to make sure that your settings are correct and selected the right mate- rial option. If you are not using the Cricut Design Space, this is easy to forget. When you utilize the software, there is a broad selection of tools to choose from. However, when you are only using a cartridge, the materials are limited. Still, regardless of which

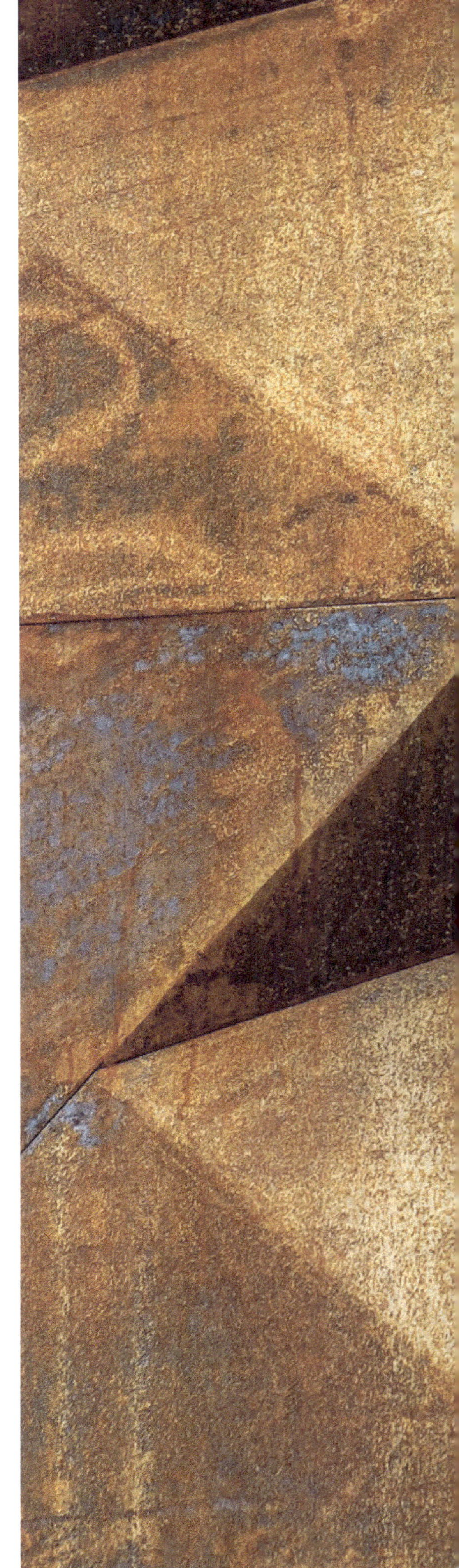

set-up you wish to handle the design, you should check your settings twice. If you are feeling paranoid, recheck them to be sure. It's easy to ruin a mat by not doing so. Trust me; you have lost more than one carpet because of forgetting to inspect my machine's setting.

Keep Your Blades in a Good Condition

Preferably, get one for every material that you are going to cut. In the list of available materials to add to your Cricut purchase, you may see different kinds of blades available. Ensure that you have the right edge for a particular item and that it is sharp at all times. A dull knife is never a good thing, and it will ruin your project as easily as a sharp one will cut it correctly.

Extend Your Markers' Shelf Life

Keep your markers upside down with the cap-covered tip facing down when you are not using them. This will ensure that they stay nice and inky for the most extended period. Please do not leave them in your

Cricut when you are not using them. Secure the cap and put them away afterward.

Register to Cricut Accessibility

If you want to get the maximum from owning a Cricut Research Air two, we then advocate subscribing to Cricut Accessibility. It's possible to pay a monthly charge of about $10, or even a yearly fee that proves to be marginally cheaper a month.

Cricut access provides you access to 30,000+ images, 1000's jobs, and more than 370 fonts. If you're likely to use your Cricut a lot, that can save a great deal of cash than if you should get every undertaking and picture separately.

Plus, it is less of a hassle to cover a set rate than stressing about just how much cash you are spending on projects! It provides up! Make your money's worth from your Cricut by creating excellent Design Space jobs.

Maintain Your Cutting Mat Covers

The cutting mats Include a Plastic shield. This may be pulled away and place back easily.

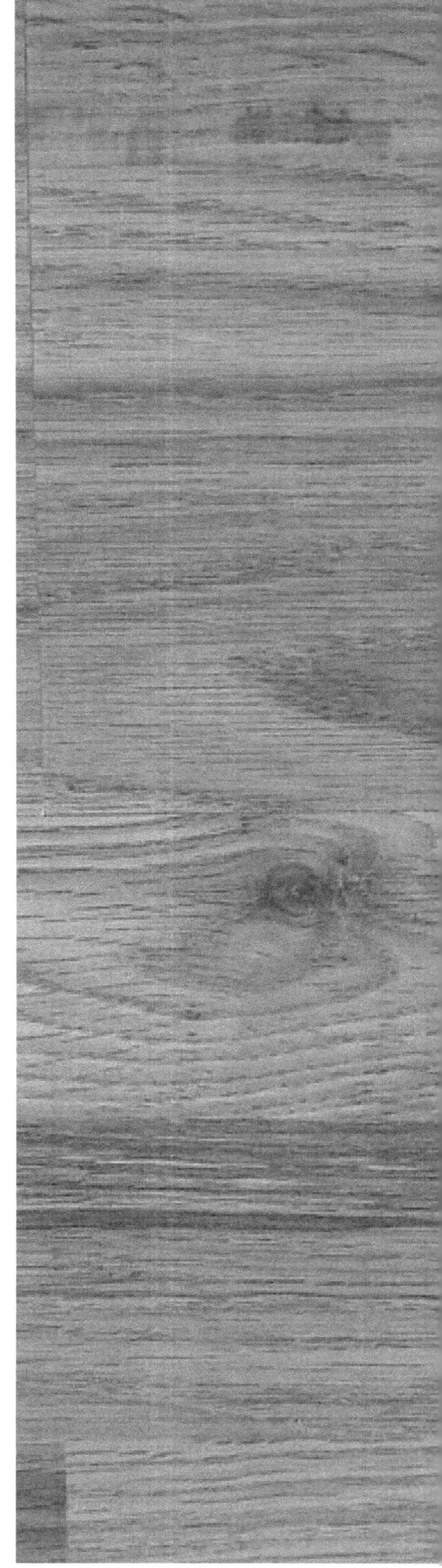

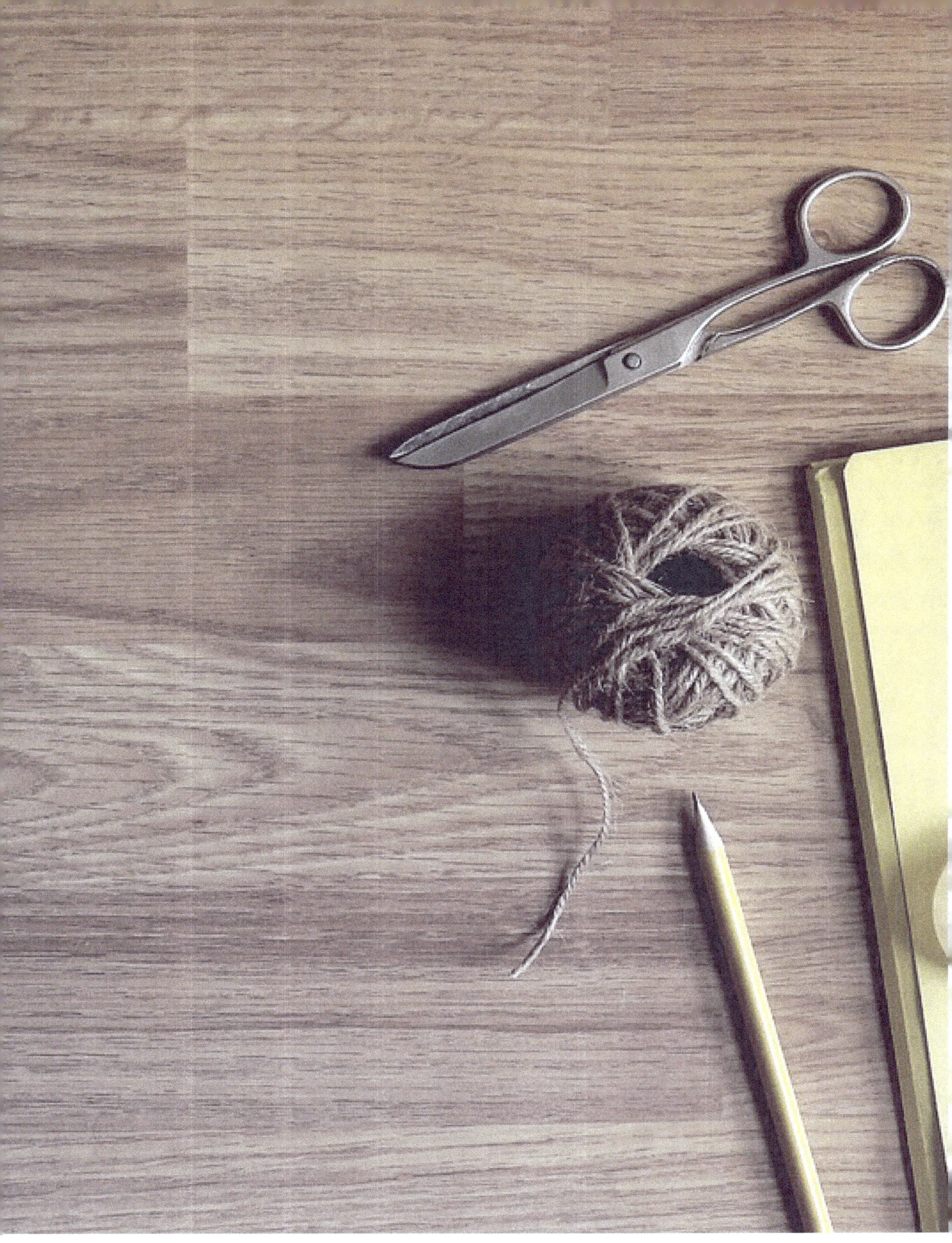

We maintained our pay and put it back on our mat. Once we are done with this, it retains the mat tacky and clean longer!

Fixing the Cricut Cutting Mat

Every once and a while (or every time you use it), provide your cutting mat a wash-over with a few baby wipes.

The non-alcohol water packs without aroma are the greatest. This can help keep it free from using cardstock and plastic residue out of cutting-edge and the typical family dust and lint drifting around.

Get the Ideal Tools

It includes a useful instrument, also a scraper, tweezers, a spatula, along scissors. It's particularly beneficial to have the wedding tool if you're considering cutting adhesive plastic or heat transport vinyl.

Start with The Sample Project

Once your device arrives, begin with the sample job.

The research air two and maker include

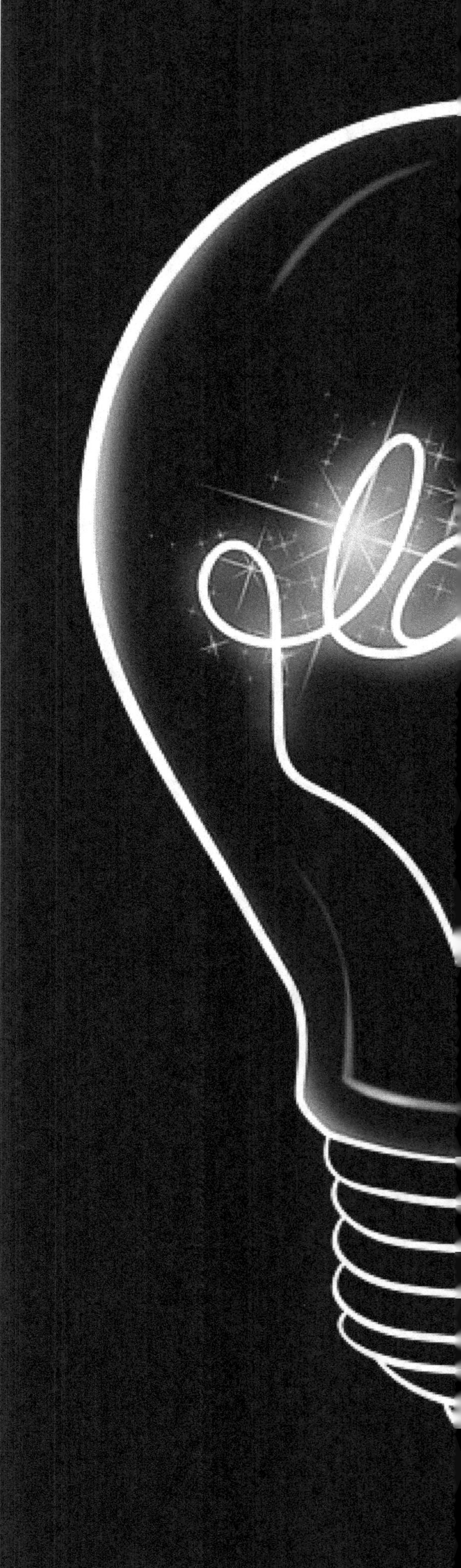

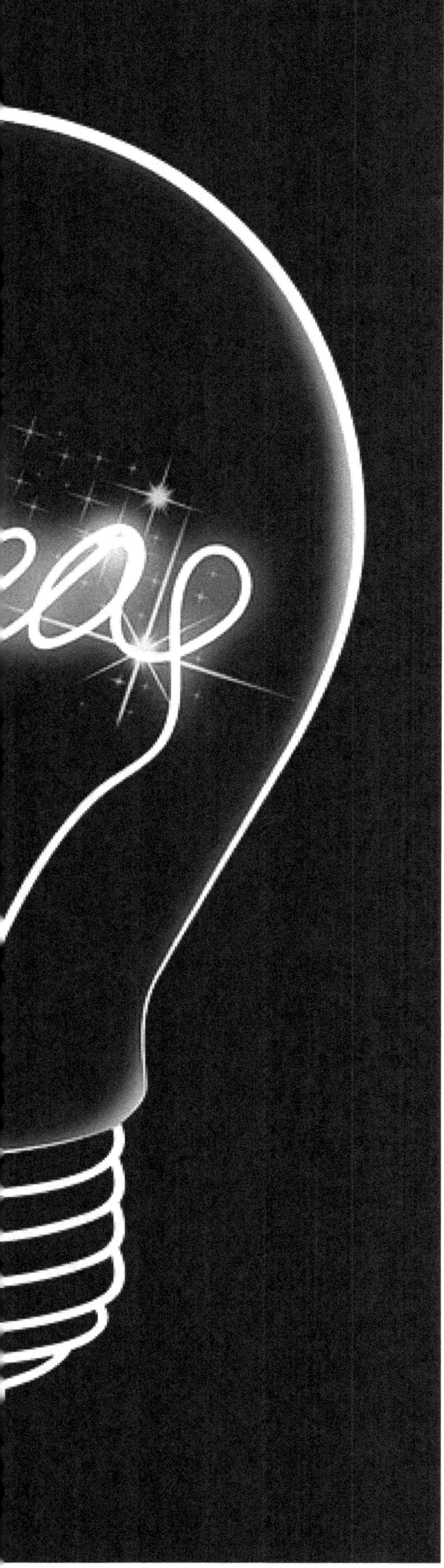

sample stuff for an initial job. Unless you purchase a Cricut Bundle, you get the minimum number of things to do this small thing. However, it is ideal to begin simply! Instead of attempting to do anything big and elaborate, start here to find a sense of how things work, software and hardware-wise.

Evaluation Cuts

After doing your jobs, it may be sensible to perform a test cut before doing the entire thing. If the blade has been set too low, it will destroy your cutting mat. When it's too large, it might just cut marginally during your vinyl, cardstock, etc., and mess up your materials.

Doing a test trimming may involve asking your system to cut a little circle. Check the atmosphere is correct and make adjustments if needed.

After Pen Lids after Utilization

It is essential to have the lid Asap after using it not to dry out. They're too costly to waste. The neat thing about the Design

Space jobs is that it frequently prompts one to set the lid back!

Aged Cricut Cartridges

Do not forget to hook up any older Cartridges you might have obtained from a former device to your account. This is a relatively straightforward process, as displayed below.

Each chance can be connected after, so if you are looking at purchasing some second-hand, affirm that this has not been achieved yet!

Besides utilizing the right tools to eliminate your cardstock or plastic in the top mat, there's just another trick to getting off it.

Rather than peeling your project from the mat, which could lead to curling (or overall mangling), peel away the rug from the undertaking. Bend the carpet from the card instead of the other way round.

Purchase The Deep Cut Blade

There is nothing worse than placing your heart upon a project and then finding you do not have the ideal tools!

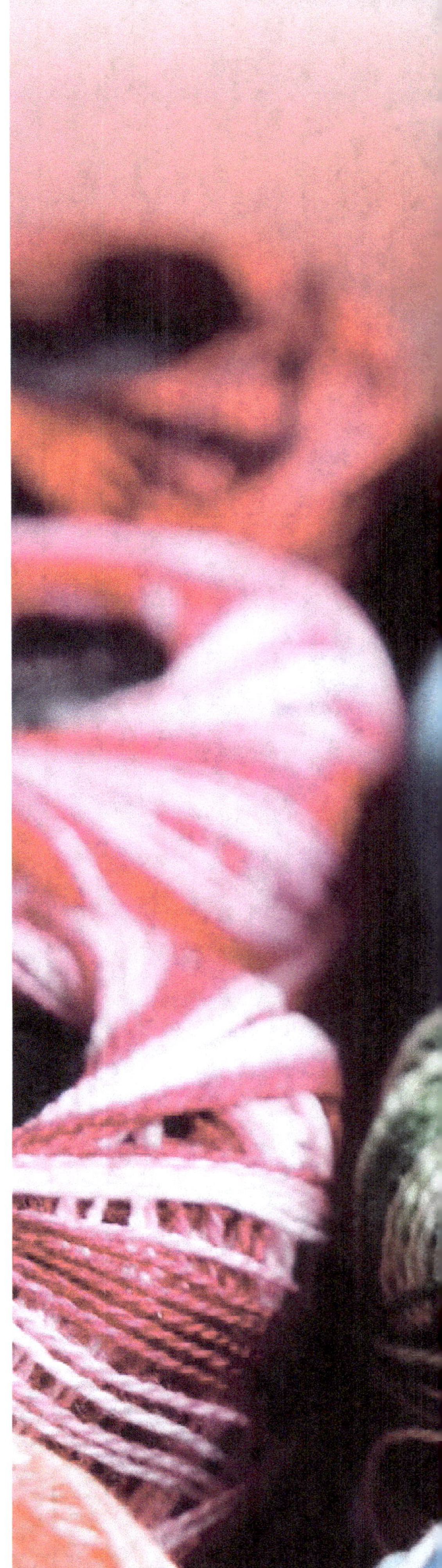

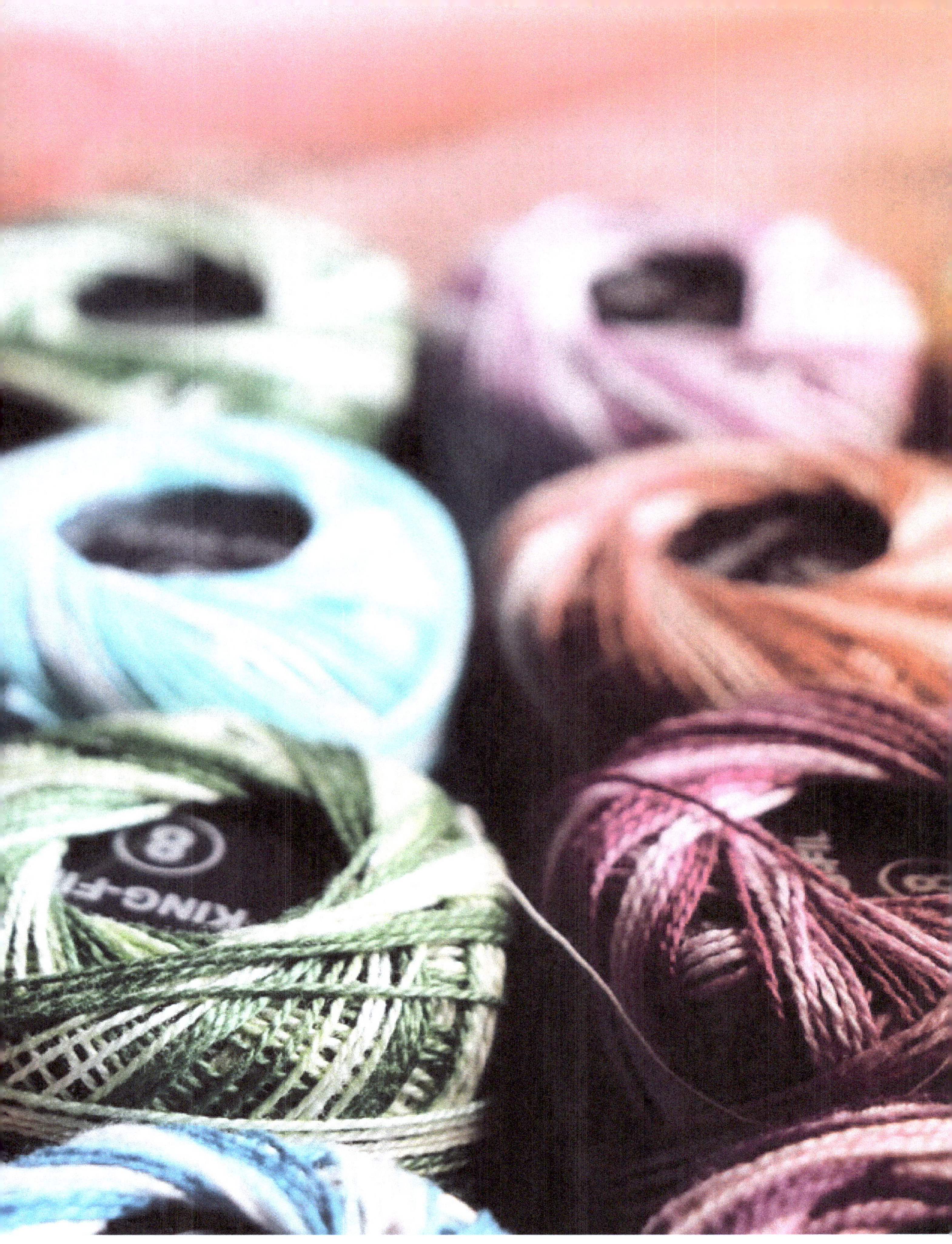

The heavy cut blade lets One cut deeper leather, card, chipboard, and much more. This blade works with all the Explore Air 2. It's necessary not just to get the edge but the blade casing too.

Alternative Pens for Cricut

You are not stuck just with Cricut Pens in Cricut Machines!
You may use Cricut pencil adapters (such as that 1) to utilize any pencil with the Maker or Air Conditioning 2. Look at these Cricut Etsy Finds for much more weird and Terrific inventions for Cricut!

Load Mat Correctly

Ensure that your mat is filled in the right way before you begin cutting. It ought to slide beneath the rollers. Your device will probably start cutting ahead of the grid's cap onto the mat or perhaps not if it has not been loaded directly.

Utilize Free Fonts

You will find so many free font websites for

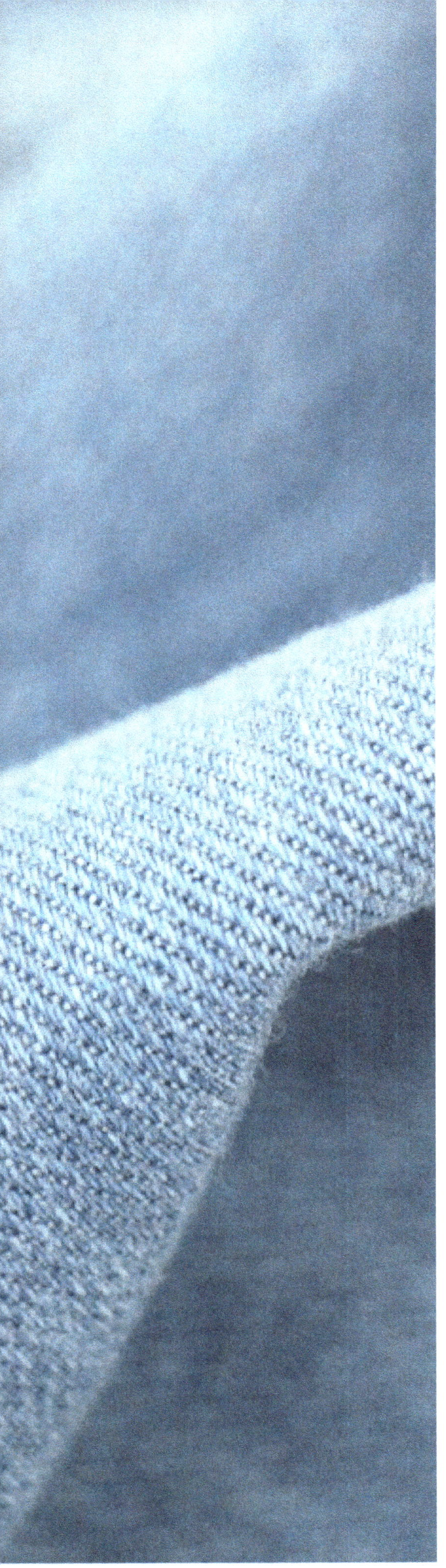

one to begin using!

Browse the internet to get a listing of free fonts for Cricut. You only download the font and install it on your computer, and it'll appear on your Cricut Design Space (see next tip).

Regrettably, among the most awesome fonts, Samantha Font isn't readily available free of charge; however, check that connection to learn where you can get it to get the very best price!

Installing Themes

After installing a ribbon to your computer, you might want to sign up and back to Cricut Design Space before your font will appear there. You might even have to restart your pc for it to appear (mine would not occur without restarting my pc).

For more information, read the way to set up fonts from Cricut Design Space.

Fixing Blades

Cricut blades utilize out if the reductions are no more so smooth and powerful, it is time for a shift. Other Indicators that you Want a brand-new blade to comprise:

- Tearing plastic or card
- Lifting or pulling vinyl off the backing sheet
- Not cutting all of the ways through (ensure your trimming setting is right too)
- You can buy brand new blades on Amazon or see Cricut Blade Guide for much more purchasing choices.

Cricuts Custom Cut Settings

The Explore Air two includes seven preset Choices on the dial:
- Paper
- Vinyl
- Iron-on
- Light cardstock
- Cardstock
- Bonded fabric
- Posterboard

If the material you're cutting is not on this listing, there's a customized option that you'll be able to pick on the dialup. Visit Design Space, choose your project, and click "make It." Then you will have the ability to select your content by a drop-down menu.

Or you may produce c new custom-made cloth. You may find mcre info relating to it on Cricut's site.

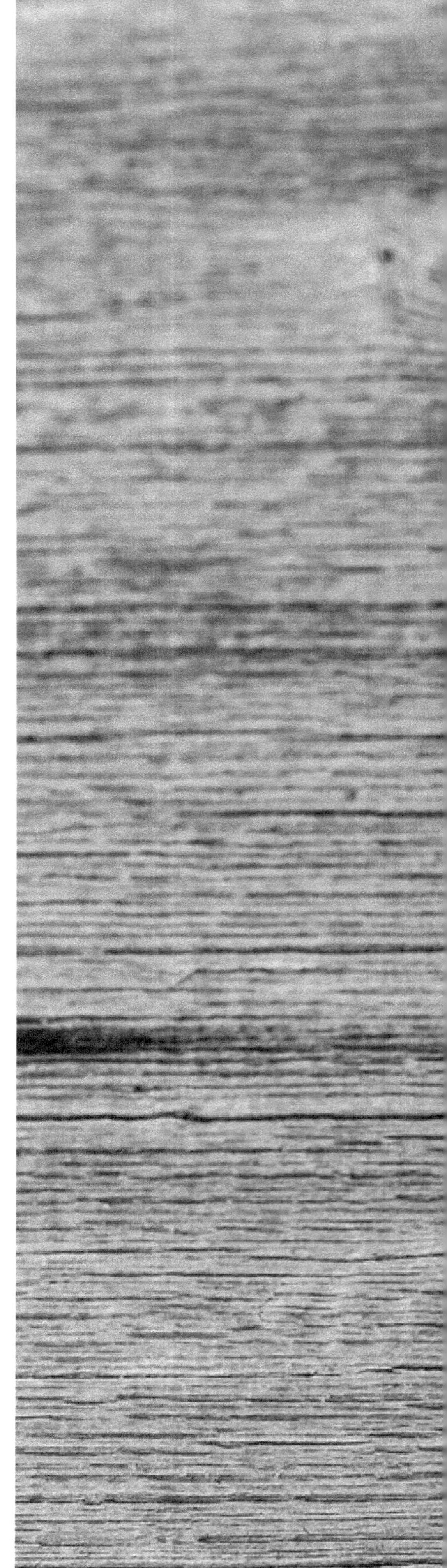

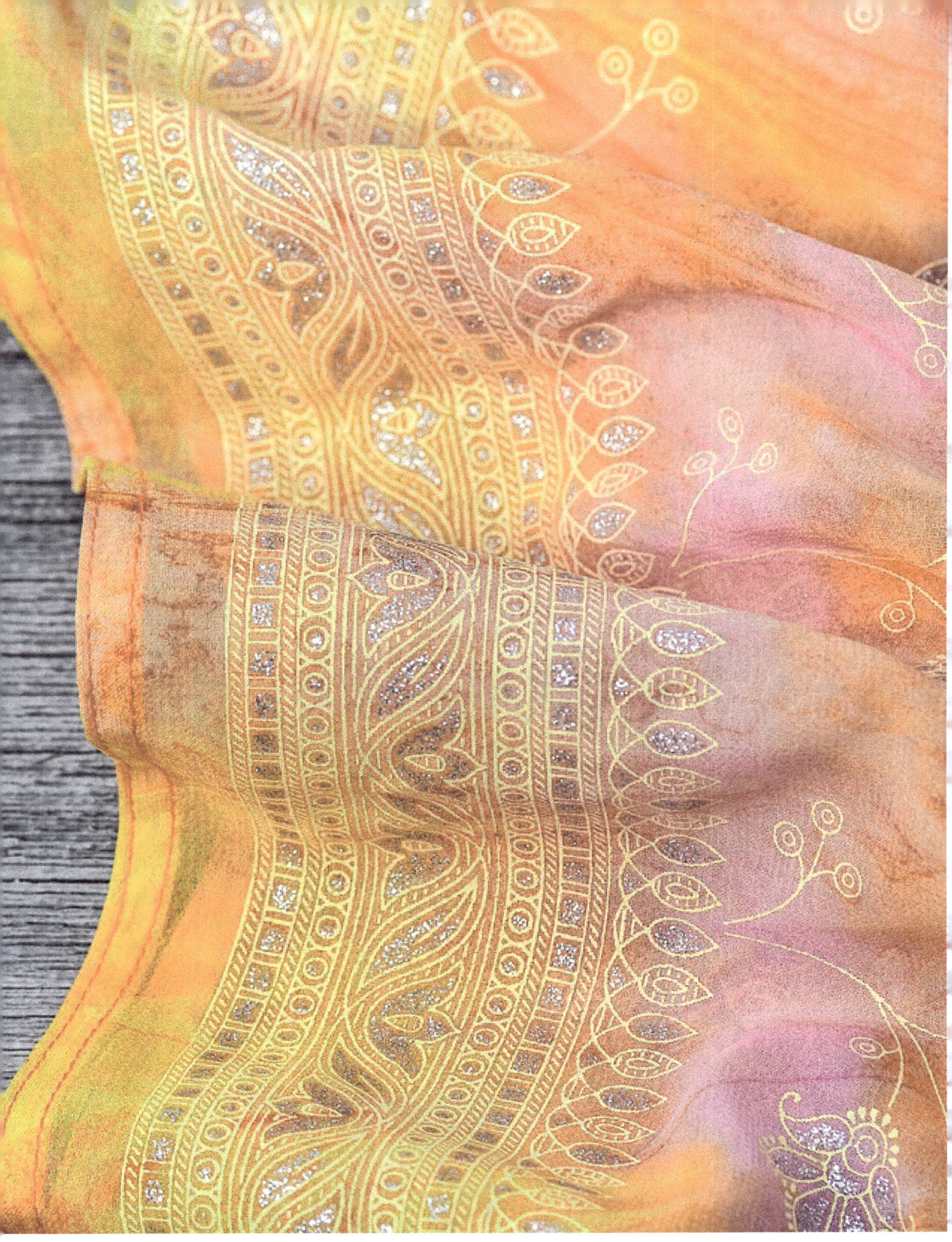

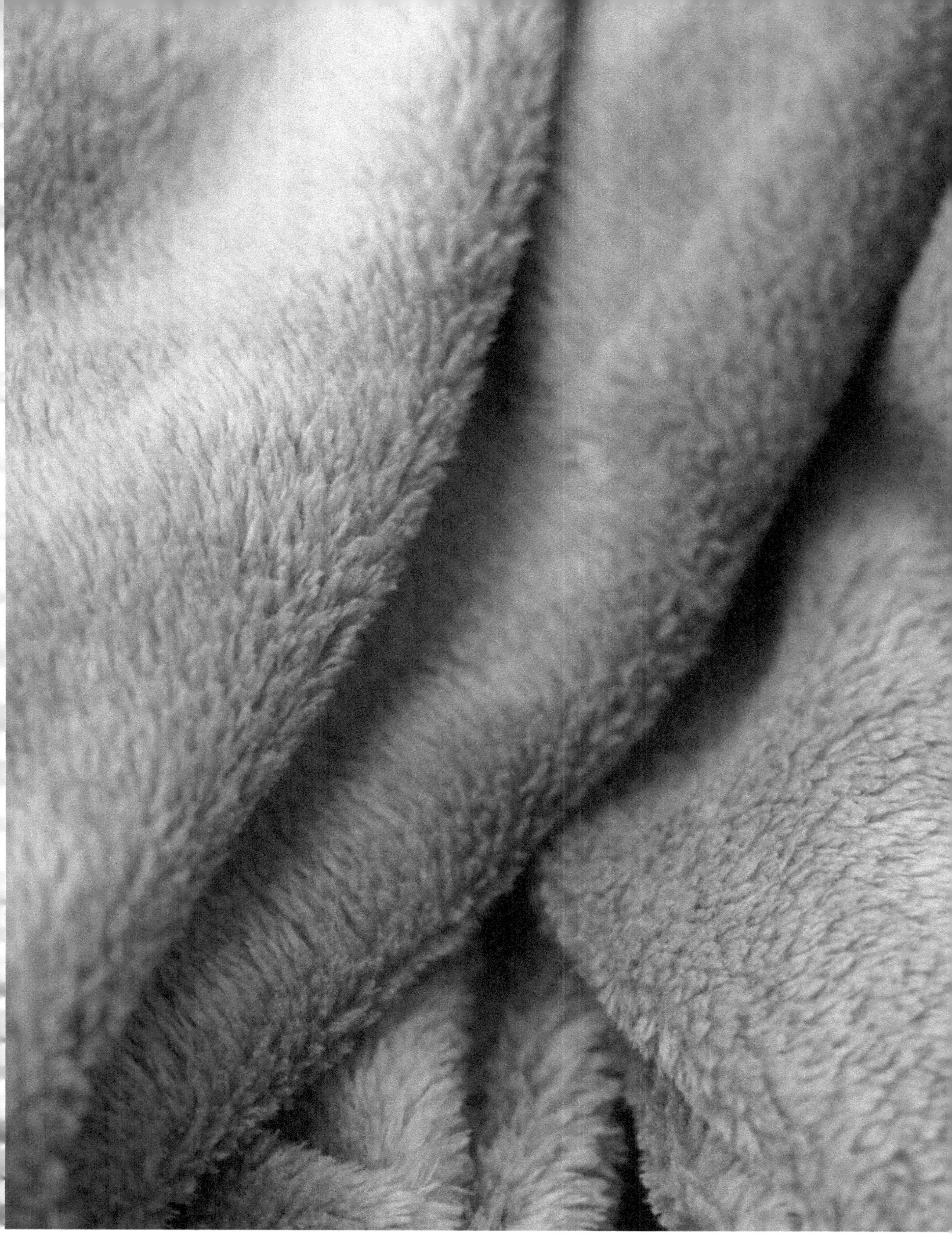

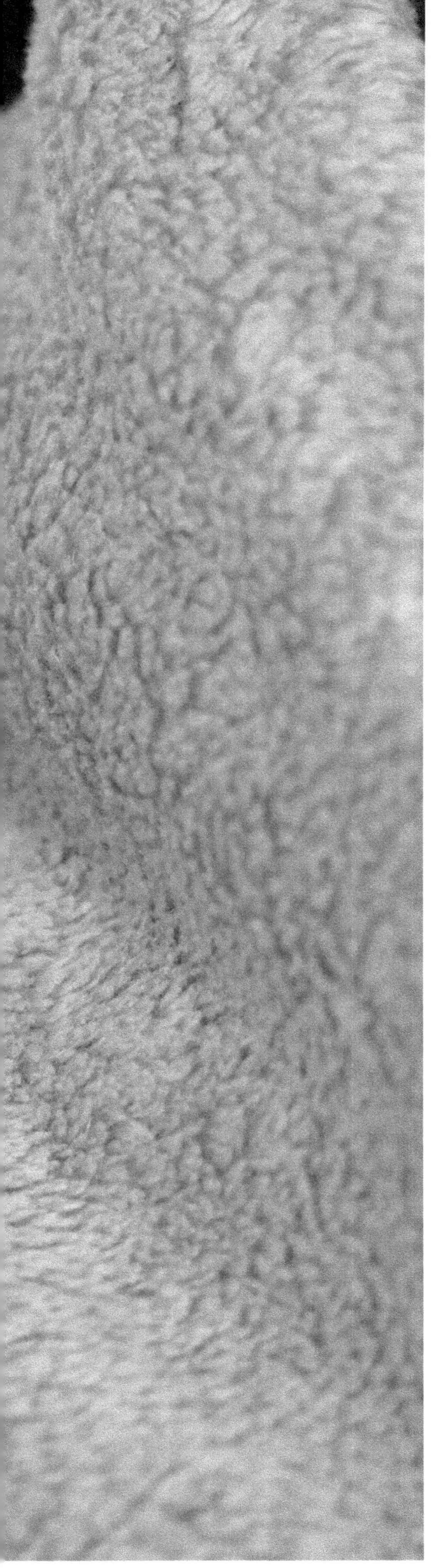

Various Blades for Different Materials

Some folks swear by using different Blades for cutting every substance.

By way of example, using one blade, which you merely use for cardstock, and yet another that you only use for the vinyl. That is because there is a variety of stuff you will wear otherwise on your blades. Cutting plastic is more straightforward on edge compared to the cutting card.

Having a committed blade to get vinyl means that it will remain sharp and ready; instead of having a blade to get all that immediately goes dull, then lifts your vinyl!

Mirror Your Pictures For HTV

If you're cutting heat transfer vinyl together with your Cricut, then you'll have to mirror your design!

Once you choose 'Make It,' there's a choice to mirror your layout (as seen below), and you'll need to pick this choice for every individual mat!

<u>Set HTV The Perfect Way Up</u>

To lower heat transport vinyl, you'll have to set your polished vinyl side down on the outer mat.

This way, the carrier sheet is. Beneath along with the dull plastic side is at the top. It is difficult to determine which side the carrier sheet is around, so remember polished side down, and you are going to be OK!

<u>Weeding Boxes</u>

If you're cutting a little or intricate layout, or you're cutting a lot of unique designs on a single sheet of vinyl, so it can help use weeding boxes.

Use the square instrument in the Cricut design room to put a box around your layout and set both components together. Unlock the silhouette at the bottom left corner manipulate it in a rectangle.

This makes weeding easier than weeding several layouts simultaneously on the one sheet of vinyl and even more straightforward than attempting to observe where your arrangements are cutting them out individually

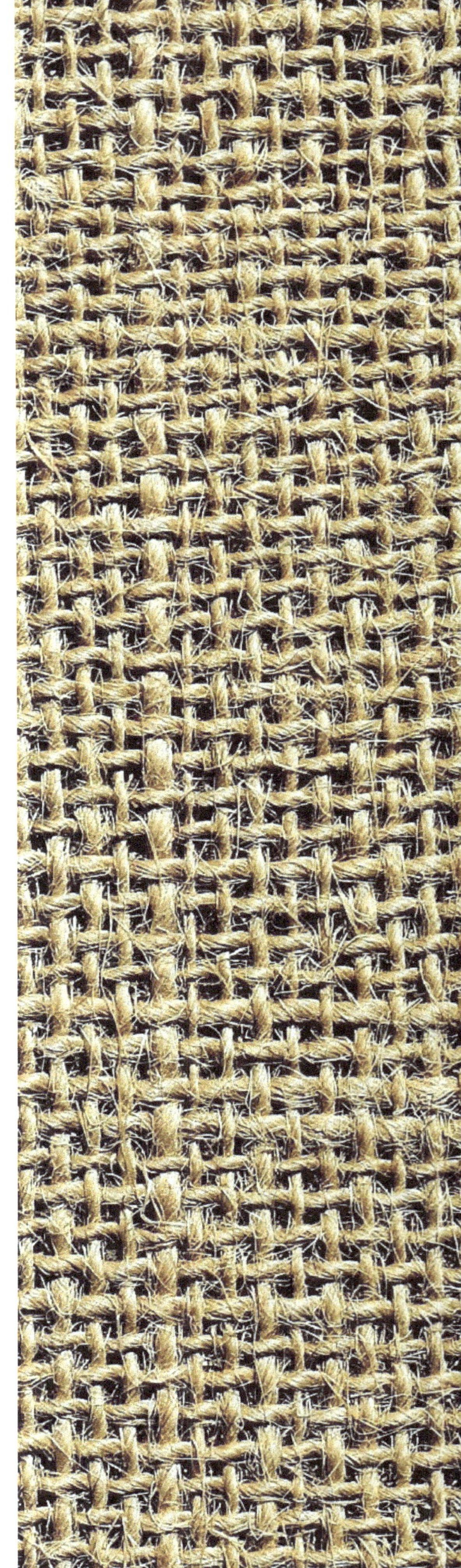

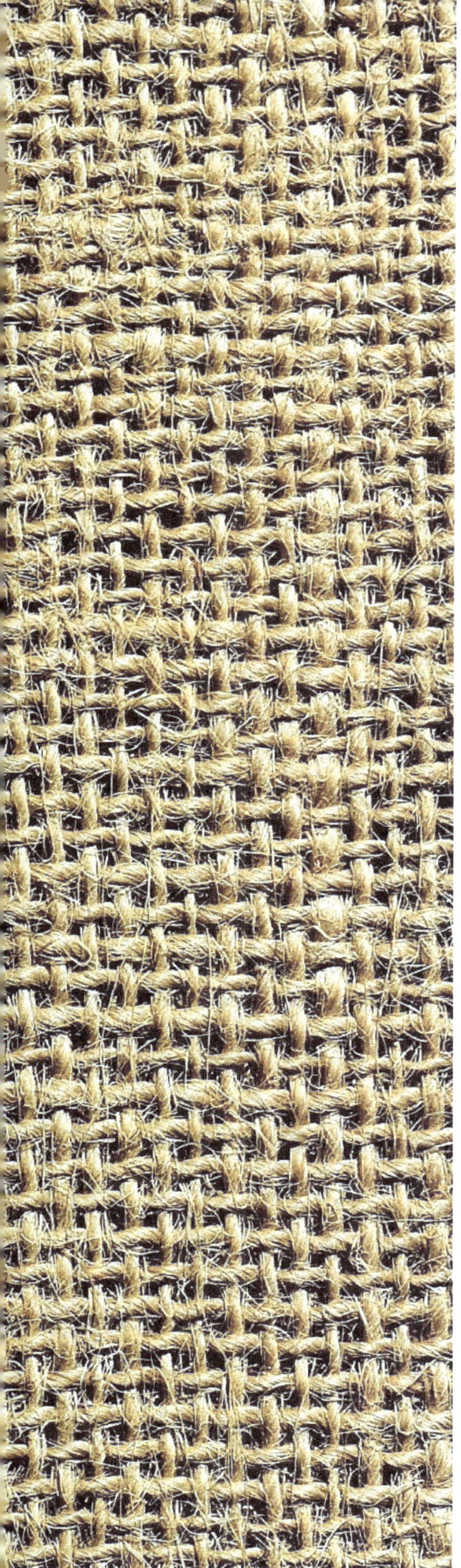

using scissors.

Extras

Cricut has a complete cutting guide on their website, which makes cutting your materials more comfortable. Reading that also reduces wastage of materials when you are testing your projects.

You can use Glad Press 'n Seal as a transfer paper to replace those expensive, original sheets. It is a cheap alternative that works well. The designs shift just as well as they would other materials.

You can use those pen grips that you don't use anymore to adjust a pen and allow it to fit into the pen grip of the Explore family and the Maker machines. The dollar store is a great place to find them if you don't have any lying around the house. You can also utilize the grip of an old pen or even elastic bands to alter the pen's size until it fits snugly in the unit.

If you find that your mat is too tacky in that same breath, you can always gently tap the carpet a little to wear the stickiness out a bit or rub it on your clothes. Just be cautious of pet hair because that will not be easy to get rid of. If you do end up ignoring my warning and making this mistake, the lint roller will do an excellent job of removing the hair. It might not get all of it out, but it will help significantly.

If your blades are dull and you need to stretch out their shelf life a little, crumble up a piece of aluminum foil until you have a proper ball. Poke the blade into the ball and pull it out again. Repeatedly do this technique for a while so that the edge will have extra few cuts in it. You can repeat this regularly to keep the blades nice and sharp and ensure that you get the best results every time you cut. The quicker your edge is, the cleaner your cuts will be. This is a cheap hack with something that you already have at home.

Furthermore, you can use a lint roller to remove those little pieces from your cutouts that might just take you all day to remove by hand. It might not snag all of those pesky bits, but the tool will reduce the number of fragments that you will have to pluck out manually. This is also helpful for removing excess glitters from your project so that they do not fly around the entire house and give you headaches for years to come (yes, we all know terrible glitter is). As mentioned earlier, it is also great for removing hairs from

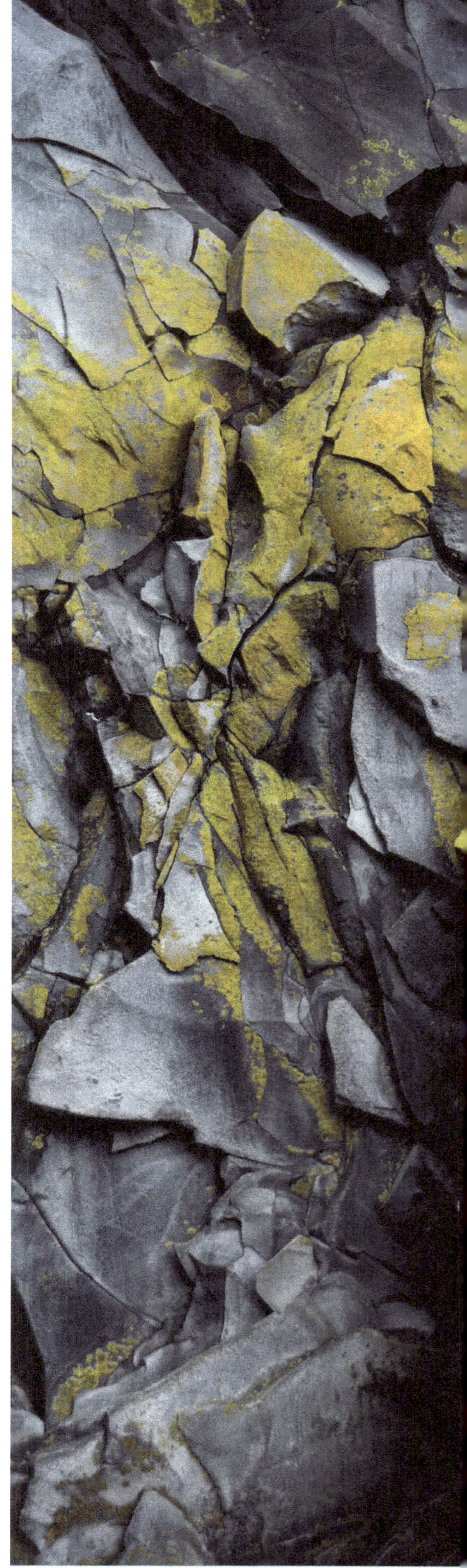

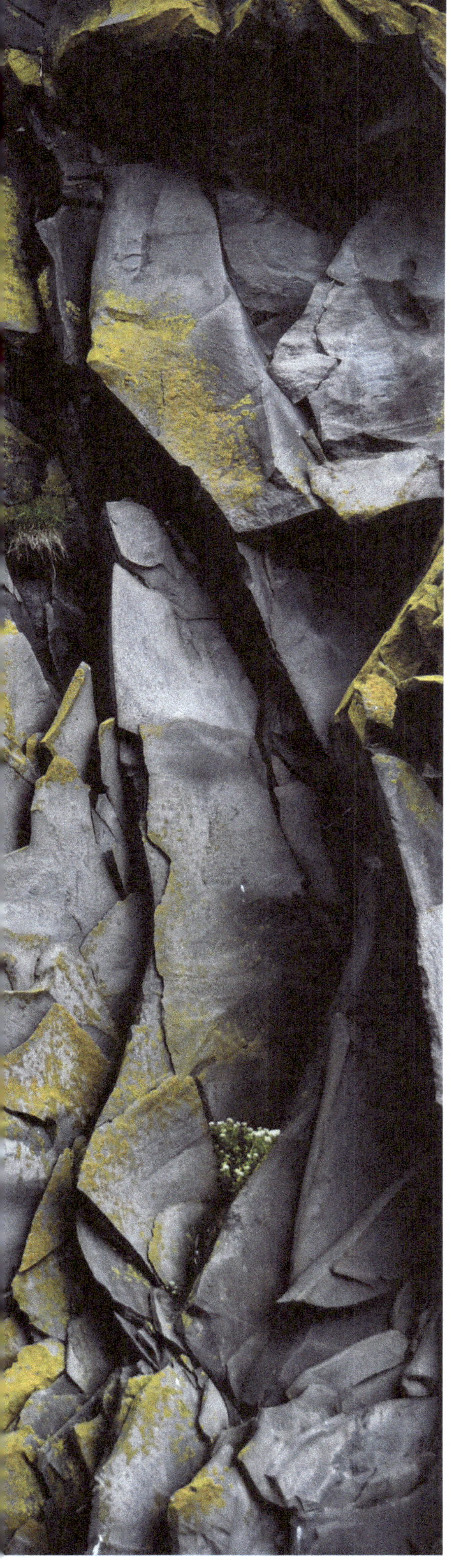

projects as well as mats.

There are communities on social media that are great for novice and advanced Cricutters. You can ask any questions, and the members of the community will do everything they can to help you as they have been beginners too. Everyone is super lovely in these groups, and you won't make a mistake if you decide to join any of them. It might be useful to have one-on-one conversations with people, too, since they might be able to help you more if they can personally interact with you and tell you what to do as you are doing the project It would help if you never left your Cricut machine open for an extended period. This will allow dust - or pet hair - to make its way on the rollers or blades. When you know that you are done using your machine for the day, close the top and bottom lids to prevent unwanted gunk from sitting on your stuff. If you want to work with white material and dust on the rollers, it will transfer onto the paper, and you will have to clean the rollers before redoing the project.

Conclusion

Here we are at the end of your reading. But not of your learning journey. I hope I have contributed in some way to learning new cononsciences and little tricks to help you with your crafts. Here we are at the end of your reading. But not of your learning journey. I hope I have contributed in some way to learning new cononsciences and little tricks to help you with your crafts.

Never stop doing research. Never stop trying new things. Never, ever stop being creative. The Cricut does not make you any less creative; it makes it easier to focus your valuable time and efforts on more important things or personalize the projects after making the cuts. It takes the tedious work out of your hands and makes everything fun, easy, and fast.

Cricut Machines make all projects and tasks related to cutting, tracking, and precision manufacturing simple. They give you the liberty to create any project, be it papercraft to vinyl decals.

All you have to do is connect your tablet, smartphone, or computer to a Cricut computer to get your project up and to run. There are various Cricut models to choose from if you're considering buying a Cricut for your home or business.

Everything on earth needs maintenance, including Cricut machines. These machines are continually cutting out materials of different textures, shapes, and quantities, etc. Thus, they need routine maintenance to boost their productivity levels and increase their life span.

The routine maintenance of these machines does not require a lot, and as a matter of fact, the hardware needs cleaning after cutting out materials. Thus, non-alcoholic baby wipes are highly recommended for cleaning material residue on the machines. The cutting mat is another item that needs maintenance from time to time because excessive usage without proper care reduces its stickiness.

When you purchase your Cricut machine, you will be excited to get started. Search the online Cricut library for ideas on creating cool projects that will make your environment more enjoyable and a project that you can use to give others joy in their life, such as cards and wooden signs.

The great thing about the Cricut is that you can use it with so many different materials that you will never run out of ideas for crafting and creating beautiful gifts.

Never stop doing research. Never stop trying new things. Never, ever stop being creative. The

Good luck with all your cutting projects.

Thank
you !!